MENTAL SPACE

Salomon Resnik

MENTAL SPACE

Salomon Resnik

Foreword by
Riccardo Steiner

Translated by
David Alcorn

London
KARNAC BOOKS

IAK

First published in Italian in 1990 by
Bollati-Boringhieri editori s.p.a., Turin, Italy

English edition published in 1995 by
H. Karnac (Books) Ltd.
58 Gloucester Road
London SW7 4QY

British Library Cataloguing in Publication Data

Resnik, Salomon
    Mental Space
    I. Title
    616.8914
    ISBN 1 85575 058 9

Printed in Great Britain by BPC Wheatons Ltd, Exeter

To Herbert Rosenfeld,
for his teaching and his friendship

ACKNOWLEDGEMENTS

I would first of all like to thank Professor Ophelia Avron, whose interest in my research work led to the invitation to give the original series of lectures in the Sorbonne, on which this book is based.

My gratitude goes also to the actor Phillipe Avron, with whom I have over many a long year discussed "theatrical space", "mental space", and life itself.

I am indebted to the postgraduate psychology students and those fellow psychoanalysts who accompanied me on these travels along the pathways of the mind, especially Simone Quelin whose careful revision of the original text did much to render it clear and comprehensible to my listeners.

I was very moved when I read the introduction by Riccardo Steiner. It was written from a friendly, syntonic, critical, warm mental space. He is able to speak about my mirror image, from another mirroring point of view as it were; in this way, through an intense and lengthy dialogue between us, he can see what I cannot always see by myself. We are never entirely alone, for being in touch with one's self is part of a complex network of inter-relationships. I thank him for helping me once again to see myself through the looking-glass of a friendly eye ("I", as Bion would have said)—from I to I, from person to person, from a friendly questioning that is part of the transference not only in psychoanalysis but in life itself. I am being helped by looking at myself, in seeing how I look to others, from an-other point of view. Probably the mystery of real dialogue has to do with the capacity to bear otherness and constructive criticism.

I am indebted to David Alcorn who, with friendship and respect for my thinking and my feelings, was able to translate this book so accurately and creatively.

I am grateful, too, to Cesare Sacerdoti, for his stimulating and rigorous attitude as a serious publisher, allowing me to speak in English to my English public. I want also to thank Klara Majthényi King for her excellent suggestions at the copyediting stage of this book.

And, finally, I think with gratitude of those who shared my company in the "cafe on the corner" after each lecture, and in the coffee-houses of my life . . . I want especially to thank my wife, Anna Taquini Resnik, for our continually stimulating exchange of views in our daily life, dialogue, and setting.

CONTENTS

FOREWORD

Riccardo Steiner, Ph.D.

Writing a preface to a book by Salomon Resnik has its paradoxical side. Inevitably, whoever writes it introduces and fixes his own impressions, thoughts, and reactions, either positive or sometimes even critical, which seem to contradict what is, in Salomon Resnik's theoretical and clinical work, perhaps the most specific (but also the most elusive) characteristic, the one that is the most difficult to determine and define: his mobility—that continual dialogue with himself, with the patient, with the real and potential public of his listeners and readers, creating by accumulation a dense "free" network of thoughts, analogies, and quotations, but also of feelings and emotions, through which—in a way that sometimes, at first sight, seems a little confused and disorganized—Salomon Resnik reveals to us what is for him his way of working. This is the case in this book, which is, to be precise, a collection of lessons on psychotic experience. But the title itself tells us that it is a question

of experience of living and communicating rather than of
lessons in the traditional sense that is usually given to
this term, even if the author has happened to speak in
an illustrious centre like the Sorbonne in Paris. In these
pages, therefore, it is possible to find the pleasure of an
encounter, of a dialogue that seems never-ending and that
moves even outside the lecture-theatre to the cafes and
streets where Salomon seems always ready to stimulate
his own curiosity and that of those around him more
deeply, often starting from simple, tiny details: a name, its
etymology, a gesture, a certain feeling, a reaction picked
up at birth, during a session or a conversation, an
unexpected memory, which the author then elaborates,
develops with very subtle attention to the characteristics
of his way of working with psychotic patients—attention
to what he calls the atmosphere of the session, to the body
and its emotional life, the unconscious experience we all
possess of it, and the way in which an empathic echo is
recreated through the body and mind of the patient and
that of the analyst. In addition, there is a special type of
attention that often leads him to very original observations on the way of living, of experiencing time and
particularly space, both physical and psychic. From this
point of view it is difficult to find in contemporary psycho-
analytical literature anything like that which Salomon
Resnik is capable of observing and bringing to life for us.
His contributions, and these pages, too, bear witness:
they are the expression of a culture that is both psycho-
analytical and psychiatric, but above all bound up with
the human sciences. I would call it almost omnivorous: it
mingles pre-Socratic and oriental thinkers, poets, and
philosophers of every age, but especially those linked with
the surrealist experience, writers like Borges and Italo
Calvino, both of whom were personal friends of the author
at different times in his life. All this, and much besides,

spontaneously interacts with Salomon Resnik's teachers: Pichon-Rivière, Melanie Klein, Herbert Rosenfeld, Bion, who was bound to Resnik by a very intense friendship, and even D. W. Winnicott, and then Frances Tustin, not forgetting a certain influence of Lacan. The reader will, for example, find in these pages some very important obser- vations on the role of the parental couple as well as of the father, which also recall the contribution of the French school. This is not surprising, in view of the really far- flung and cosmopolitan nature of Salomon Resnik's education: from Argentina he went to Paris, then to London and back to Paris, but he also spends time now in Italy—Venice, especially, is one of his favourite "sanc- tuaries", where he can rest and meditate.

What also strikes us in this book is Salomon Resnik's particular sensitivity to the bond that can unite the plastic arts, especially painting, to the psychoanalyst's work. This is not surprising, given the type of patients with whom the author works, and his interests. Certain problems linked with the ontology of existence, with gravitation and levitation in space, the possibility of self- expansion or of feeling totally crushed and suffocated, feeling oneself living in time or feeling totally blocked and petrified, are of basic importance in the pathology of the dream-world and in the hallucinations of psychoses and can easily find a visual correspondence in certain art, such as that of Bosch, Magritte, Mirò, Klee, de Chirico, Van Gogh, to name only a few. But the most striking is Salomon Resnik's instinctive capacity for recourse to painting as though it were a dream—an auxiliary dream, aesthetic and made in the presence of reason, to help us understand better through illustration not only his patients' experience, but also his own. There is an aesthetic sensitivity, a poet-ego and a painter-ego, in the way Salomon recounts his patients' cases, which distinguishes him almost exclusively among his colleagues, even those more illustrious than himself, who are occupied with this field of research. And for those who know him and know how he moves, how he speaks also with his body and his gestures, these pages hold an almost graphic trace of his personality, which sometimes recalls those characters in Chagall's paintings who seem to levitate in mid-air, as if guided by hypersensitive antennae to receive messages that are invisible or based on psychic ultrasound, but without completely losing contact with the earth, even if at times they seem fascinated by the joyous nature of their levitation.

Some of the most beautiful and interesting pages of this book, then, are those devoted to the use that Salomon makes of certain masters of contemporary painting in order to clarify the experience of his patients. But what is also important is that Salomon Resnik's observations are transformed often into the possibility of new, original readings of certain masterpieces of Magritte, Van Gogh, de Chirico, and so on, without ever falling into those terrible biographies based on the pathology of the artist to which so much contemporary psychoanalysis has accustomed us.

I should like to emphasize one more thing before finishing. From these pages, as from others of Salomon Resnik's work, there shines forth a sort of empathic and sometimes almost affectionate respect for the suffering of the patient, whom he always seeks to individualize, to perceive as a person; and he is also helped by his deep knowledge not only of psychiatry, but also of philosophical phenomenology. To this is added a sort of modesty, which is almost always there in Salomon Resnik's relationships with the patients for whom he is caring. In comparison with the arrogantly paternalistic and patronizing tone of so much contemporary psychoanalysis—in which the analyst is too often transformed into a sort of "psycho-agogue"—a teacher of the psyche—or in which experimental science, which seems to triumph today even in our field, basically reduces the patient to a "thing", forgetting the person—these pages should teach us all to remember a famous Latin saying that seems to condense many aspects of Salomon Resnik's work: "*homo sum, nihil humani a me alienum puto*"—"I am a human being, and I consider nothing belonging to humanity as alien to me."

London, 1994

PREFACE

From my early childhood, my dream was to have a room to myself. My family was of modest origin, and it was impossible for me to have a room of my own until early manhood. In those days, I would walk at night along a wide and well-lit avenue with lots of movement, lots of life. In that Latin city which is Buenos Aires, the coffee-bars were open until very late at night. I used to go there and meet young poets and thinkers, some of whom were trying to find themselves, whilst others were so terribly lost in the world around us. As a young adolescent, I would identify with them. One day, walking along the street, I experienced solitude in the crowd, solitude while I was with people—a discovery of a place inside myself in which I could experience syntonically my own intimacy. Thereafter, I would go alone to coffee-bars where I knew nobody, in order to think by myself, to write, to experience my generation contemplatively.

When I left Buenos Aires in 1955 for the first time, I was already a doctor of medicine and a psychoanalyst, and I was about to attend my first international congress of psychoanalysis. It took place in Geneva, and I went there with Doctor Enrique Pichon-Rivière, David Liberman, Professor Ostroff (who was both philosopher and psychoanalyst), Leon Grinberg, and Dr Alvarez de Toledo, who was my last analyst in Argentina and to whom I am deeply indebted. In Geneva I met Melanie Klein, Winnicott, Bion, Herbert Rosenfeld, Hanna Segal (whom I had already seen in Argentina during one of her seminars), Jacques Lacan, and all those psychoanalysts whose writings had so interested me. I was very moved when I met Mrs Klein, and I said to her that sometime within the following two years I would like to come to England to attend her seminars and, if possible, to have further analysis with Herbert Rosenfeld.

I returned to Argentina, became a full member of the Institute of Psycho-Analysis, and prepared my own mind and my patients for dealing with separation and mourning. I was making ready to jump into another space, a very attractive one for me—Europe (my parents came from Russia). Attractive, yes, but what a frightening experience. I did not have the means to go directly to London, and besides I wanted to experience an intermediate space—Paris, the city of light of my adolescence. My own culture—and, indeed, my psychiatric training—had so much to do with France and its civilization. I spent a year there, working with Doctor Georges Daumézon, a major figure of the great French school of classical psychiatry. I was able to do some work with schizophrenic patients in his ward, which was of interest to him; when Professor Morris Carstairs came from London and asked Dr Daumézon if there was any innovative research in schizophrenia being conducted in his hospital, Daumézon put forward my name. I had to speak French with Professor Carstairs—my English was so very poor. He suggested I come to England; I replied that he was like an angel bringing the good news I was so eager to hear: I was hoping to be recommended for a post that would allow me to be in London. The answer came within a fortnight: two hospitals were willing to offer me a consultancy. I was able to "emigrate" to what I felt to be my predestinated place.

England was the right atmosphere, upsetting but stimulating, in which to go back to my basic solitude—to re-discover and go further into my own mental space. I was impressed by Melanie Klein's paper on loneliness (1963), and later by Winnicott's "The Capacity to Be Alone" (1958a).

* * *

In another of my books (Resnik, 1986), I wrote that real dialogue is an encounter between lonely people—or, rather, between people able to be alone, people who are neither invasive nor overwhelming nor seductive, people who can give "solitude" to each other. I use "solitude" here to mean a living loneliness—being alone with oneself.

The subject of this book is really my ontological preoccupation with discovering this creative solitude within myself and being able to help my patients both to gain insight into themselves and to recognize that there is more space for feeling and thinking creatively than they thought. In dreams this often appears as a closed door to the attic or to the basement, which, once opened, leads to a vast space, sometimes empty, sometimes stuffed with the accumulated rubbish which so often we use for filling up a hollow barrenness.

To find a place to be oneself is an adventurous experience that everyone desires, yet we live in a culture

where we are always running away from ourselves—
but running away only increases the fear of finding oneself, and the fear, in turn, increases the tendency to run
away, to escape into the outer world. Sometimes, in the
adolescent mind (whatever our chronological age), this
appears as the compulsion to jump into the mind or
the mental space of a guru or some other leader. When I
jumped into Europe, I had to face this in myself, the
identity problem of going towards a great and idealized
analyst and philosopher—Maurice Merleau-Ponty, for in-
stance, whose pupil I was in Paris. I was facing in myself
the identity problem of any young person who is becoming aware of his need for an ideal ego but at the same time
has to avoid the alienation of extreme idealization and
must go back to his own ego ideal and "real" ego.

One day, after writing this book, I found in a bookshop
Virginia Woolf's *A Room of One's Own*. I was struck by the
title and felt very much in tune with her language and
evocative metaphors. Virginia Woolf gave me the living
image of the idea of searching for a space for oneself. She
awakened in me my infantile and adolescent romantic
feelings of wandering around gardens and houses, woods
and flowers, the need for some warmth inside ourselves,
which we may call "mother": the interiorized good mother.
For me, the idea of mental space in psychoanalysis is a
way of stimulating in each of us some warmth in our own
intimate houses: the body. Psychoanalysis is sometimes
a necessary mediation—as Paris was for me, between
Buenos Aires and London—which will help us to discover
our "inner home", to repair it and make it fit for living in.
The psychoanalytic process is a way of wandering inside
our own history, through the dark and the grey, and
also the light. Sometimes our inner path is obstructed
by periods of bad weather—those upsetting inner times,
which may even freeze over.

Living time in space is to flow along in the world like a river, to adopt Heraclitus's image of time being a river that changes unceasingly. Life is part of the nature of man, and the principle of all things in pre-Socratic thinking is movement, motion. To experience e-motion is a way of being alive and in contact with both inner and outer reality, where fantasy and imagination actively allow us to transform the routines of life into something magic in our world.

MENTAL SPACE

Introduction

Il n'y a pas de pouvoir divin, il y a un vouloir divin
éparpillé dans chaque souffle; les dieux sont dans
nos murs, actifs, assoupis.

René Char, *Les Martineaux*

The present text is based on a series of lectures I gave at the Sorbonne between October 1987 and June 1988. The audience consisted of final-year psychology students and newly qualified psychoanalysts and psychiatrists. The lectures were given in an amphitheatre that gradually filled with the ideas we created together, the audience and myself, sometimes silently, sometimes noisily—ideas waiting for someone to think them, as Bion might have said.

How could we integrate the medley of feelings and ideas floating in this vast composite space and arrive at some degree of harmony and unity? How were we to combine all these different points of view?

At times, the space of the hall was like mental space, with its varying degrees of cogency and harmony. On such occasions, the atmosphere was bright, pleasant, and breathable; but at other times an accumulation of floating thoughts and inanimate feelings turned it into something heavy and oppressive—a cloud obscuring all attempts at understanding. This atmosphere was mainly of my making, but the audience played its part too. When you breathe the air of feelings and ideas, changes of climate reflect the mental state of the entire group. We could think of it as an immateriality full of ideas, with as yet no apparent content, immobile, waiting expectantly. These qualitative changes in the space of our encounters are a way of expressing my feelings as I recall them now in my mind. An "empty space full of ideas" is the way I experienced the situation in fantasy; no space is literally deprived of qualities. Einstein commented that Descartes was probably correct to claim that empty space did not exist; since the discovery of electromagnetism, space, considered as a magnetic field, is always qualitatively real and "existent".

All discourse takes place in time, aiming for the future along its own adventurous path between presence and absence, following its own rhythm, with its breaks (little deaths) and instants contributing to the life and structure of the *logos*. "Little death" implies that every separation between ideas is akin to an experience of mourning. Language, either as thought or as spoken discourse, is a set of acts of weaning. Melanie Klein declared that cognition (thought and speech) arises and evolves from the work of mourning characteristic of the depressive position.

To return to the conference hall in the Sorbonne: during the pauses at the end of each lecture, students or colleagues would ask questions, albeit in a somewhat ritual manner, publicly or privately: often a small group would come with me to continue the discussion over a cup of coffee in a local cafe. Spontaneity of dialogue is often facilitated by the intimacy of a small group. Once, as we were sitting in the cafe, we debated the difference between "mental space", "internal world", and "psychic apparatus". We concluded that it would be impossible to speak of an internal world without the concept of mental space. And "psychic apparatus"? To this, Anna Resnik answered: "The mind is the all-purpose crank-handle."

The essential idea here is that of movement, the basis for every kind of change, whatever the species. The question might arise as to who holds the lever. The mono-theistic theologian might say God, but the polytheistic Greek thinkers believed that though the deities could influence both body and soul, they did not wield absolute power over man. Though man is αὐτοκίνητος [*autokinetos*: he moves by himself], he is subject to external forces emanating from the realm of the gods. Hippocrates considered the sacred sickness, epilepsy, to be a disease caused by internal factors—a disturbance in the brain, the physiological and symbolic expression of a private vital space. The origin is endogenous, but the gods influence the outcome.

During the Roman period, meetings of the *comitia* were interrupted if one of the members had an epileptic seizure [*comitialis morbus*], thought to be an expression of the displeasure of the gods. This origin has remained in the French term "*crise comitiale*" to describe epileptic fits.

The pre-Socratic philosophers believed that the movement of the planets corresponded to the discursive rhythm of the universe. Heraclitus considered the *logos* as a virtuality; Parmenides added that in order to *become*, one must first *be*. These two perspectives may be complementary, in that it is necessary to stand still for a moment in order to think about becoming. A pause, a little death, with its solitude and separation, enables the individual to take stock of his world. In his *Theatetus*, Plato argued that becoming and the idea of movement [from the Latin *motus*: emotion] are fundamental elements of mental and physical life (Resnik, 1985b). Much later, he described existence in terms of movement, sensation, and knowledge. Comparing hot and cold, wet and dry, he debated the question of sensory perception, the difference between things as they exist in the world and their "appearance" or fantasy. He considered pleasure and sorrow, desire and fear, colour, sound, and movement (rapid and slow) to be a phenomenology of the body experienced in a world as yet virtual. Depending on the moment, one's eyes must be open (waking life), or closed (sleep and dreaming); to which must be added the dreamlike reverie of the poet.

What is the meaning of reality in this ever-changing life? The external–internal landscape is like a kaleidoscope, whose intermittent discontinuity moves from hiatus to pulsation. When Plato debated the question of fantasy and reality in the myth of the cave, he imagined the prisoners coming out of their inner life (the cave) carrying with them the shadows that would become fantasies only when projected onto the mirror surface of the river.

The screen on which images are projected is always mobile. The flow of water is a screen par excellence, thanks to which feelings can be given expression.

This book is a study of the vicissitudes of the psychopathology of everyday life as manifested in clinical material drawn from my experience as a psychoanalyst with neurotic and psychotic patients through their daytime and nocturnal fantasies. Freud observed the spatial dimension of reality with nocturnal eyes to adjust himself to the visible opacity of the unconscious and, like the prisoners in the cave, to give shape to fantasies and knowledge—that is, to express them in the clear light of day.

The mind is like a musical instrument—a lyre that, in spite of its as yet imperfect tuning, can evoke the Ancients. The notion of *Stimmung* in phenomenological psychiatry is derived from *Stimme*, voice, and *Stimmer*, the craftsman who tunes an instrument. We could borrow the metaphor and say that the therapist's function is to help to tune an instrument that is not quite in harmony, not completely in tune, more or less discordant. The psychotic experience, which does not always imply psychosis *per se*, plays an important role in Klein's concept of the individual. My own interest in metaphysical and existential questions leads me to pay careful attention to the psychotic aspects of the non-psychotic individual. In order to understand psychotic experience, we must be in contact with the everyday ontological concerns of people and their interrogations about life and death. When a patient's affects have been blocked for a long period and his "soul isn't moving any more", the re-awakening of time hitherto immobile and paralysed may be felt as a catastrophic experience. This is what Bion meant when he talked of catastrophic change occurring during the psychoanalytic process.

Serena, a young schizophrenic woman, would speak of herself in a cold, impersonal manner; in one session, she said: "I'm suffering from an *etherotopic delusion*." I had understood her to say *heterotopic*, and, though unfamiliar with this particular psychiatric term, I felt it to be phonetically and conceptually interesting. I asked her what the expression meant (thinking of the Latin *hetero*, other). Her answer was very simple, but quite different from anything I could have imagined. Following her private philology,

Serena explained: "*Ethero* is derived from ether and means that since I was suffering so much, I needed to put my brain into a container full of ether."

This was Serena's way of showing me just how useful her delusion was in resolving the problem of how to create for herself a mental space within that vitally important organ (her brain); her intrinsic fragility made it impossible for her to face up to life's difficulties in a way compatible with her mental condition. As her mind awoke, the ether started to evaporate; Serena began to feel and to think in a creative way, though the poems she wrote were filled with immense mental pain. Her experience of life was immediately enhanced; time, which used to be paralysed, began once more to move forward; and her sheer desire for life became so imperious that I had the impression she was trying to make up for lost time.

One day, while Serena was in the clinic, a nurse found her attempting to commit suicide by hanging. Later, she declared that she did this because she wanted to live. In the following session, it became clear that her desire for immediacy in life was so urgent that she wanted to live "a century in five minutes" and then die. Like Achilles, "swift of foot", who chose to live a short but glorious life, Serena wanted to live the life of a legendary heroine, however narcissistically destructive it might turn out to be. No matter how arrogant the ego, it must face the painful problem of tolerating the possibility of change. This "catastrophic experience" of existence bears witness to the intensity of some situations of psychotic liberation.

The discovery of insight is sometimes a vertiginous revelation for the self as it awakens during the psychoanalytic process and discovers or re-discovers its own mental space, which had hitherto been denied or ignored. To discover that there is a space for feeling and thinking is often experienced on the phenomenological level as a void or a bottomless pit. To acquire inner perspective, to lean inwards from our own window, can be like falling blindly into the unfamiliar dark abyss of unconscious reality.

For Freud, self-observation calls on that part of the ego which during the psychoanalytic process can project itself into the psychoanalyst's eyes as into a mirror and then look upon itself, poised between fascination and pain. Bion used the term "vertex" to refer to the visual pyramid observing the intimacy of its own being, like the Aristotelian νοῦς [nomos] looking down from on high at man's seemingly bottomless chasm. To reflect on insight is an experience of overwhelming emotional intensity. The soul for the ancient Greeks, the mind for Freud acquires wings when repression and denial are lifted, and it can either accept its condition of being intimately bound up with the body in a universal actuality (the mind and the body ego are two sides of the same coin), or it can leave the body and fly off to live its psychotic escapades through other bodies, personalities, or cosmological constellations (metempsychosis and metasomatosis) (Resnik, 1986).

Melanie Klein's concept of projective identification contains an element of evasion and reaching out to other mental spaces in a gradient that goes from normal to pathological. The more persecutory or pathologically depressive a given life experience is, the greater the need to separate from our own body ego by splitting mind from body. Some degree of splitting is part of normal life—indeed, being constantly aware of one's body may itself be pathological, for example in hypochondria—but excessive splitting gives rise to complex psychopathological conditions such as depersonalization or split personality and threatens the very unity of the self.

In his *An Outline of Psycho-Analysis*, Freud (1940a [1938]) wrote: "We assume that mental life is the function of an apparatus to which we ascribe the characteristics of being extended in space. . . ." The psychic apparatus expands to occupy space according to the rhythm of each encounter. The psychoanalytic experience is a dialogue with reality, which requires the transference and its upheavals for its very existence. In the transference, both patient and analyst face themselves and each other—two people in dramatic encounter, two minds coming closer yet remaining apart and observing not only the landscape of the other's mental space but also that of his own: *autoheterocontemplation*. The psychoanalytic dialogue, sympathy, empathy, antipathy, apathy—all are different metamorphoses of *pathos* in this encounter between mental spaces. Between narcissism and the capacity to tolerate otherness, the models of childhood emerge in the transference. The parasitic model, for example, is given dramatic force in the necessity for the one to live inside the mental space of the other, who is to be wholly responsible for the treatment; the symbiotic model expresses itself as reciprocal parasitism. Ontological insecurity demands that pathos be projected into the mental space of the other, which can then be used as a nest. The inability to inhabit one's own mental space gives rise to the metempsychotic need (projective identification) to take possession of that of the other.

To listen means to leave space for the other to speak and to allow oneself to introject his projections. One of my patients, Miss Olga, complained that her mother never had any time to listen to her or any space for her, her head was so full of television soap operas. But in the transference, this patient quite often could not listen to my remarks because she was absent-minded (absent from her mind) or, perhaps because she felt threatened by the environment, afraid to leave any space open for another person.

The role of the psychoanalyst is to remember his expertise as a former patient and to help his analysand (the *alter ego*) acquire that same expertise. In his craft, the analyst has to call upon his knowledge of the workings of his own mind; his own mental space becomes a research instrument enabling him to get in touch with the cacophony of his patient's emotional experiences, or their eradication.

Philosophers and psychologists have tended to ignore the fact that there exists a space outside the body; yet every body must occupy space, as Paul Schilder (1935) argued in his pioneering work in the field of psychoanalysis. He wrote of a primitive or primaeval space, not yet unified, which on the emotional level is expressed principally via body apertures. It is difficult to describe one's own space; to differentiate between the distances internal and external objects occupy with respect to oneself is a complex subjective task. The cultural environment may refuse to recognize the spatial reality of the body in its sexual dimension or as a body–tomb [σῶμα–σῆμα: *soma-sema*). When we accept the idea of the body, we have to accept the fact that it has boundaries; the space in which we live is limited, and at the end of time we come up against a wall. To live is to accept the passage of time and the finitude that is our future. Anaximander, refuting the notion of infinite time [ἄπειρον: *apeiron*], put forward the hypothesis that both space and time possess form and limit. In his attempt to conceive of the primary form of the body and its elements (air, water, and fire), he became involved with the form of time, nature, and the cosmos— that is, with geography and cosmology. He was, in fact, the world's first cartographer, the first to give shape to reality and to history. Later, Empedocles was to add the fourth element, earth. The universe was inhabited by unknown forces called gods, who could take on human or animal shape in the myths. The universe of myths is like a collection of fragments, parts [μοίραι: *moirai*] of the global space whose essential feature is to be linked together.

In Greek and Roman polytheism, the gods are the bearers of man's feelings. The unconscious too is fundamentally polytheist—we need only consider its diversity of agreements and antagonisms. For Freud, the capacity for belief and idealization, for sanctifying the things we venerate and hold in awe, is part of the cartography and topology of the structure of the unconscious. The ego ideal (an ideal of oneself) searches for an ideal ego (the Other). This Other, in Freud's view, is the father, but for Melanie Klein—as I argued in one of my articles (Resnik, 1989)—it is the mother. Freud spoke too of parts or pieces or fragments of the mind [*Stücken*] as constituting a complex three-dimensional cartography of the psyche.

Melanie Klein established the third dimension—a stereoscopic view of reality—through her notion of internal objects and a three-dimensional ego living within the mental space of the internal world, as opposed to the two-dimensional concept of an image projected onto the flat surface of a screen. Similarly, in the present book, I attempt to describe mental space as a geometrical and physical reality that is constantly in movement, in the same way as post-Euclidian geometry conceives of a three-dimensional world evolving with time—i.e. quadri-dimensionality. In his book, *The Unconscious as Infinite Sets*, Ignacio Matte-Blanco (1975, p. 418) says that when we dream, we contemplate a multi-dimensional world with eyes made for three dimensions. The idea of multiple dimensions came to Matte Blanco through his reading of Freud's dreams. When we dream, we become multiple personalities, experiencing our adventures in time and space simultaneously through each of the protagonists. I, too, speak of dreams in this book, for in psychoanalysis the interpretation of dreams is the royal road thanks to which we are able to familiarize ourselves with reading and understanding the messages of the unconscious.

It is not easy to accept one's mental space, for the laborious task of memory, reminiscence, and knowledge in general is bound up with a feeling of mourning, as Freud and Melanie Klein pointed out. One form of defence against the difficulty of accepting one's own inner space and multiplicity of being consists in filling up the available mental space—with thin air, a vacuum, or even with erudition. The paradox is that erudition and experience— even *in materia psychoanalytica*—can be used to fill up the space for feeling and thinking or as a smoke-screen for refusing to acknowledge its existence.

The illustrations in this book are paintings and drawings by established artists or by some of my patients. They are an attempt to encourage the reader towards an aesthetic and sensori-perceptual experience of the unconscious. I am grateful for this material and particularly to my patients for the help they gave me in fulfilling the difficult but exciting task I set myself.

I began this introduction with some comments about atmosphere, about being able to breathe or feeling stifled, about warm and cold, wet and dry, as applied to the mental space of our encounter. I close with this acknowledgement, that when something is too complex and difficult to make intelligible with words, the artist is there to give it visual form and content.

A space for psychoanalysis

I intend this chapter to be a first attempt at creating dialogue between us, an exchange of views between my mental space and yours in order to generate a space between us. I hope that the clinical material drawn from my practice as a psychoanalyst, together with sketches made by some of my patients and paintings by established artists, will help us to get closer to those aspects of our experience which, because they are intangible, are difficult to share.

Freud was fascinated by the work of artists and poets, for he believed them to be in intuitive contact with what remains concealed, repressed, or forgotten in everyday life. Obviously some consideration must be given here to the cultural context in which he was formulating his theories—*fin-de-siècle* Vienna—and to his ties with the intellectual and artistic life of the time.

In his biography of Freud, Ernest Jones (1953–1957) relates that when the philosopher Ludwig Klages, a friend

13

of Freud's, was asked what was the best way to study and understand Freud's thinking, he replied: "By reading Freud." Jones himself says that the best way to understand the historical development of Freud's theories is to read his writings in chronological order. I recall that when I began my training in Argentina, students were required to read Freud sequentially during their first three years, in much the same way as medical students read anatomy.

Yet reading and quoting from a writer's work is no simple task; every reading is, in itself, an interpretation. Whenever I quote Freud or those of his pupils with whom I worked in London, I cannot avoid interpreting; my mind, my thoughts bring their own influence to bear on the words I read. The text is a domain over which my thoughts and intentions meander to extract a particular meaning, which I can then offer for your consideration (in Brentano's sense of "intentionality"—we know that Freud attended Franz Brentano's lectures at the same period as Husserl). We could say that in his own way Freud was a writer, a poet; see, for example, his "A Disturbance of Memory on the Acropolis" (Freud, 1936a). The etymology of the word "poetry" shows us its links with creation and invention. Freud was a discoverer and explorer who tried to set down what he experienced. He attempted to communicate what he had discovered through clinical material and the practical application of his hypotheses. His research on the activity of the mind, the concept of the unconscious, the meaning of dreams, psychopathology, and artistic creativity is intimately connected not only with his own experience of life, but also with his clinical practice. I, too, use clinical material in order to share with you my own experience as a psychoanalyst and to try to acquaint you with a certain number of theoretical concepts that I consider essential.

But, first, what is theory? It is a way of looking at things, of experiencing certain phenomena. In ancient Greece, θεωρία [*theoria*] meant looking, seeing, observing, contemplating—and, hence, speculation. Festugière, the famous scholar of ancient Greece, declared that the primary meaning of the word θεωρία refers to seeing [θεωρεῖν: *theorein*], looking at landscapes, and implies the idea of marvellous (Festugière, 1936). Plato refers to θεωροί [*theoroi*] in the sense of exploratory journeys to far-off lands and seas.

If philosophy is a reflective experience of contemplating the world, the psychoanalytic adventure is an internal contemplation that enables us to look into ourselves and discover what has been excluded from consciousness. To help us do this, we require someone else, because psychoanalysis is an experience that concerns relationship. It is this that makes the notion of transference so important: something is transferred from one to the other, from patient to analyst and vice-versa—what in psychoanalytic terminology we call transference–countertransference. In an earlier book (Resnik, 1986), I suggested the idea of "double transference" in order to emphasize the fact that psychoanalysis is a sphere in which each protagonist takes something from the other and induces something in the other. Bion, with whom I trained in London, used to say that the way in which the patient perceives the analyst is very important; the further removed from authenticity the patient is, the more he requires to develop a semiology, a code for deciphering the other. It is important, too, for the psychoanalyst to understand how he is perceived; hence the idea of inter-dependence inherent in the very concept of therapy. (The term "therapist" is itself very ancient; in ancient Greece, the "therapeuts" were those who took care of the gods. It appears to desig-

nate some of Moses's followers, but was also applied to
the Essenian sect, the Jewish contemplative order at the
time of the Second Temple, whose task was to provide
support and relief to anyone in difficulty. Philo of Alexandria describes them as a paleo-Christian sect.)

The psychoanalytic experience has to do also with the
idea of investigation; each of us has his own individual
world, inhabited by a kind of internal family, a universe of
objects to be visited during the analysis. Mental space
and internal world exist only if the world can be perceived as having three-dimensionality (see Laplanche &
Pontalis, 1967, s.v. "Phantasy"; see also Ferenczi, 1909;
Isaacs, 1952). The psychotic often lives in a "deflated"
world, a flat landscape without hills or valleys, with no
space for emotions or thoughts. Feeling, thinking, imagining—these require internal illumination; Paracelsus
declared that the ability to imagine was the sign that an
internal sun existed.

To return to the question of theory and praxis and our
discussion of the concept of transference: Freud was bor-
rowing an idea from Plotinus and the neo-platonists when
he referred to the man within and to the impossibility of
dissociating the inner self from the external world. This is
precisely where the idea of transference comes in—part
of this dynamic exchange with significant others is
reproduced in the dyadic context of the psychoanalytic
relationship. What we call "insight", the contemplation of
our inner world, the discovery of what has remained
hidden from consciousness, is not something that occurs
in isolation: it is impossible to analyse oneself as though
all that were required is to look in a mirror. Freud himself
emphasized the limitations of self-analysis.

The mirror, however, is an appropriate metaphor when
we refer to the development of imagination. For Winnicott
(1958b), the first mirror we know is our mother's face

when we look into her eyes; it is a very special mirror in that it reflects not only the baby himself, but also what the mother is feeling. For Melanie Klein, the creation of an imaginary world (psychic reality) is in itself a relationship experience, and the transference originates in such infantile experiences in the early stages of development (Klein, 1952). The term "transference", as I have pointed out, takes on a specific meaning in the psychoanalytic setting, precisely because of the fact that it has to do with relationship. It is for this reason that in psychoanalysis the concept of mental space is not synonymous with internal world; it includes the external world and interpersonal communication with others.

In the psychoanalytic experience, theory and practice are inter-dependent. Within this reciprocity, the analyst's craft and the patient's expertise grow together. Metaphorically speaking, if psychoanalysis is a skill (just like any other), the patient, too, has a task to do, and he has to learn how to do it. Psychoanalysis is ongoing training, further education; when someone strives to be truly himself in his social, family, or academic relationships, he has to develop his own way of doing things, not imitate others. From that point of view, analysis is a process of identification—I shall come back later to this highly complicated issue.

The psychoanalytic relationship is not built simply on the words spoken; it includes the atmosphere generated by a certain type of presence. Good things and bad things are deployed, depending on whether the atmosphere is one of empathy or of antipathy—but if there is apathy, absence of *pathos*, then there can be no movement, and nothing can occur.

Reaching out towards someone for the first time, in the first session, creates a kind of tension. A transference fantasy is already taking shape as the patient makes his way to the analyst's (in the street, the café, the bank). The analyst also experiences some degree of tension, an expectancy, a countertransference fantasy—somewhere on the far side of the transference, or on the other side of the street. The horizon is some distance away, but it may suddenly close in—we call this resistance, fear, or anxiety, in one or the other of the protagonists. The voice on the telephone asking for an appointment, the voice that answers, the exchange of letters—all this creates a context in which something is already being exchanged, it is part of the anticipation from which a relationship is born. The first session is an unveiling, the birth of something new, an exclusive relationship that will develop through time in the analysis. Anticipation gives rise to an illusion, i.e. projection of expectation and creation of an ideal. Once again we can turn to Winnicott and his primary hallucination—the "hallucinated breast", as opposed to the mother as a present and whole object. The concepts of ideal ego and ego ideal were developed by Freud in "On Narcissism: An Introduction" (1914c). Narcissistic satisfaction requires the ego ideal to be accomplished in the ideal ego. The ego ideal constructs an image or model—the ideal ego—a target that it attempts to attain. The ego ideal is always on the look-out for a "superior" or "aggrandized" image with which to disguise itself or to identify. At first, this image is narcissistic, and the supremacy of narcissism, the supremacy of an absolute and homogeneous identity principle, makes it difficult to acknowledge the other in his own right; expectations of him and idealized projections onto him may not coincide with what he really is. Authentic dialogue must be founded on the recognition that every encounter is necessarily asymmetrical; in accepting that the other is different from me, I discover the reality of my basic solitude (Winnicott, 1958a).

Given the structure of the situation, the psycho-analytic process is a voyage between illusion and disillusion. For analyst and patient to work together even when there is disagreement or when the transference is negative, the analytic process requires a setting, a space, a theatre in which the unexpected and the problematic may be worked out.

Fixing a time and a place for the sessions brings to mind the idea of "field work"—a concept made familiar by the topological writings of Kurt Lewin (1963). Lewin was a pupil of Stumpf, who had worked with Einstein. The notion of "field" belongs originally to the world of physics, Faraday's experiments, and Maxwell's theory of electromagnetism. To borrow the idea of field from electromagnetic theory, we can say that every space, even when it is experienced as a void, possesses its own specific identity and quality. Einstein himself pointed out that Descartes was correct: vacuum is also presence.

The expression "field work" is a metaphor derived from ethnology and anthropology, and as such was familiar to Freud (1912–13). Minkowski, whom Freud quotes, introduced the idea of reaching out towards the other on his own home ground (Malinowski, 1964; see also Kaberry, 1963; Malinowski, 1944). The metaphors Freud borrowed from other sciences—for example, from archaeology—are a typical component of the transference "field", though sometimes discreetly; psychoanalysis is a kind of archaeology that explores the λόγος [logos] of the ἀρχή [arkhe]—a quest directed towards the ancient and primitive, beginnings and origins.

"Field work" is a notion employed in American psychiatry, especially by practitioners influenced by psychoanalytic theories (Sullivan et al.), and in Argentina. Enrique Pichon-Rivière (1975) used to say that on closer examination of the very first meeting with a patient, we can see that all the essential imaginary ingredients both of the nervous disorder and of its cure were already present, together with the primitive or in-fantile patterns of object relations.

The idea of rhythm or tempo must also be taken into account. Rhythm requires discontinuity and pauses, and pauses are unavoidable "little deaths". A state of flux, "to become" (Heraclitus), is important, but it is just as crucial to stand still, "to be" (Parmenides), in order to take stock and reflect on the itinerary. Even if a pause is experienced as a loss, as something missing, as a mourning, it is also the ability to accept difference in the real world.

The setting, the space of the relationship, concerns the format of the psychoanalytic work. The patient is heedful not only of the surroundings and of the content of the analyst's comments, but also of the feelings the analyst communicates to him. If what we say corresponds to what we feel, even though the words may not be quite right or to the point, that is perfectly sound practice; but if there is conflict between our words and our feelings, the patient will introject a split image. Therein lies the complexity of the psychoanalytic situation; the unexpected is part of the psychoanalytic adventure, as in every other creative activity.

I think that the greatest quality a patient can acquire after a long time in analysis is ego flexibility, the ability to invent and create the analyst each time. A common language is constructed out of words and gesture, an atmosphere in which communication becomes possible (or, perhaps, impossible); there is presence, too, and a *persona*, corporeality, ways of behaving or of pretending that each of us possesses. "Reality, the unexpected", said Henri Maldiney.

I remember a story about Italo Calvino. I had asked him to take part in a symposium on creativity in Venice. He replied, "I am busy with the work of creating and inventing the novelist who is going to write my next book." The teaching of theory and technique is provisional; I, an experienced psychoanalyst of many years' standing, cannot foresee the language that will flow between a patient and myself, nor the role or roles I shall be called upon to embrace over and beyond my true self.

These considerations lead me to the theme of this book: mental space, an attempt to reclaim a *locus* for thinking about what is perceived, a *locus* that is often transformed or emptied or obstructed or deflated.

Bion, speaking about transference, used to say: "When we speak from within the transference, we bear witness." In this intimate encounter we call psychoanalysis, if the couple formed by patient and analyst are successful in their attempt to work together, then seeing, listening, and perceiving with all of our sense organs become possible. Even when mistakes occur, we can still communicate, for the ability to tolerate error implies the capacity to accept some degree of uncertainty.

With these topics in mind—rebirth, birth of self-knowledge, field work—patient and analyst endeavour to construct a framework to which we give the technical name "setting", a resourceful and enterprising workshop. Field, setting, constructing analytic space, the rhythm at which the work will be done—all are aspects of the analytic contract, which, like every contract, requires two parties.

In the following chapters, I draw on material from sessions with my patients; this is my way of inviting you into my workshop, even if only for a short time. I try to communicate some idea of the way I work, and from these clues you will be able to build up an image, an imaginary picture of a relationship between two people. Perhaps questions of theory and practice will spring to mind; this, in turn, will enable us to open up a space together, a space in which we can attempt to communicate and to build our own little—or big—workshop.

CHAPTER TWO

A space for thinking

I n this chapter I discuss some clinical material. I hesitated over this in chapter one because it was our initial contact, and we first had to get to know each other. Reaching out from oneself towards the other always entails a risk: interpersonal contact is indispensable but hazardous.

The analytic experience itself can be regarded as being replete with risk, insofar as what may occur is always different and unexpected. Given the magnitude of conscious and unconscious variables in operation, it requires, as I have said, great stability, which is why I have emphasized the idea of the therapeutic setting, the psychoanalytic situation, and the developmental history of the encounter within the psychoanalytic process.

The notions of sphere, setting, psychoanalytic space, and construction of place and rhythm for the work of psychoanalysis are the fundamental elements of the therapeutic contract. A good contract, just as in fair play, means that you can make the rules clear during implementation: it is creative, meaning that technique and schools of thought are less important than style and personal ethics. Living in a contractual society, we need to reach agreement about rules, but we have to leave some opening for inventing those most appropriate to each case.

The words we use must, at least metaphorically, reach out towards the patient's own language in the same way that in child analysis the words are the play sequences the child brings to his session. In the therapy it is essential for the analyst to maintain a playful ego, which can reach out to that of the patient, even though the latter may be limited, paralysed, or unresponsive.

Let me say a few words now about Liliane.

She is an intelligent and very sensitive woman, but fragile. My impression was that she was not very happy in her emotional life, but as far as I could judge she was not psychotic, and this is why I want to start with her case material. In Kleinian theory, the difference between psychosis and non-psychosis is relative, in that analysts do a lot of work with the psychotic nucleus in each patient, and with both psychotic and neurotic transference phenomena.

Liliane suffered from neurotic symptoms and behaviour disorders. She had a teenage daughter with whom she had a good relationship, and she was separated from her husband.

In our first meeting she told me she found it difficult to think and to do anything creative with her life; she felt destitute inside, and, above all, she wanted to be able to experience some kind of pleasure. She had great difficulty in enjoying herself or even in feeling pleased, both in everyday things such as looking at a painting and in her personal and professional relationships.

Liliane gave me the impression of being very tense: she would walk in a hurried and bustling manner. Occasionally a smile would light up her face, but on the whole she looked sad and depressed; her features would harden from time to time.

I believe it is important to describe the demeanour and attitudes of a patient. As you know, in Freud's first clinical case-study he describes the body language of his patient; it is only later in the analysis, when he explains her psychotic ritual, that this aspect diminishes in importance and he no longer has to look at her.

In her sixth session, Liliane, lying on the couch, said after a long silence: "I have nothing to say . . ." and, after a further pause: "I work very hard, and I have no time for thinking." She had already told me in a previous session: "The time I have for thinking is always employed to some other purpose." This is a characteristic aspect of our culture—keeping ourselves very "busy" in our everyday life. This is how we fill up space; a space that at times we cannot put up with. In my view, this may culminate in a phobia of existence, of our inner world, of our unconscious. Liliane always had something to do and was unable to tolerate any kind of pause. What, then, becomes of rhythm, that fundamental element of time, if there is no lull, no hiatus?

Liliane was so involved with external demands on her that she had no private space inside; I had the feeling that her innermost space was always "occupied", full of "nothing to say".

Noticing a certain coolness in Liliane's way of speaking, I asked her about her feelings. She answered: "I feel cold inside", adding: "Sometimes I feel anxious." I wondered what she meant by "anxious", and she tried to explain. Putting her hand to her breast, she said: "It's a feeling of discomfort, and it frightens me. I have the impression that I can't control it."

There is *angor* in her (in French, Italian, and Spanish, the term corresponds literally to "anguish" rather than to "anxiety"; Freud's own German term, *Angst,* has the root *ang* [to tighten], which is related to the Latin *angor* [pain]; Melanie Klein speaks of "early anxiety", and she uses the expression "depressive anxiety"—Klein, 1975). This is the transient distress that we all experience, but Liliane's behaviour shows that she is in a quasi-permanent state of anxiety and apprehension. There is a semiological difference between anguish and anxiety. "Anxiety" is derived from the Latin *anxietas*, from *anxius* and *angere* [to cause pain] and is a general description of an individual's state of being. "Anguish" comes from *angustia* [narrowness, constriction] and, as the German *Angst,* has a specific physical significance.

Liliane's demeanour then changed, and what was worrying her changed too: now she was distressed by her work. Liliane was a reader in a publishing house, and she wrote short commentaries on various authors. She longed for the appreciation of her superior, but he was often less than enthusiastic about her productions. I felt that this was her way of transferring to another context something that was, in fact, taking place inside herself. Charcot (1893) described transference as being related to body phenomena, in which a symptom refers to and is associated with another, within the same body. Freud borrowed the notion from Charcot, but in an intra-psychic, intra-somatic sense, and extended it to cover various forms of interpersonal relationships.

Liliane expressed her personal problems as if they belonged to her place of work. After a pause, she asked: "Do you understand me?" I replied: "It seems difficult for you to know if what you express, what you 'publish', will be approved of or understood by me, the therapist–superior."

This is a good example of my way of thinking about and translating my interlocutor's thoughts and feelings; Melanie Klein taught me to use in an imaginative way the word-plays the patient expresses during the session. Liliane used the term "publish"—i.e. making public what is private and secret for her—hence my use of the same word. In supervision with Bion, I learned to respect the words used by the patient and not to alter them without due cause.

After a further pause, Liliane added: "I am always tired and I have to make an effort to express myself, to translate what I am feeling." She told me of her lethargy and her feeling of mental and physical sluggishness. Lethargy and sluggishness are often expressions of "somatic" depression, to borrow a term Pierre Janet (1909) used in his description of psychasthenia.

Then, from the *soma* [body], Liliane touched her head—an attempt, in my view, to transfer what she experienced in her body to her mind: this is what thinking is all about. She added: "My head is full of political opinions, of things I have read in newspapers and magazines. But you can't keep these things in your mind, they disappear, blown away by the wind. . . ." If these things could be swept away in the wind, they are probably mere snippets taken from newspapers and not real ideas. She continued: "The wind sweeps away all my energy too; and I feel destitute without mental energy."

Here we have an opportunity to discuss a theoretical problem. The word "energy" is derived from the Greek ἐνέργεια [*en*: in; *ergon*: work], and exists in both active and passive forms, as Freud pointed out in his discussion of the idea of instinctual drives. As we know, Freud was influenced by Helmholtz and the scientific postulates of his day on conservation and transformation of energy. In "Instincts and their Vicissitudes", Freud (1915c) alludes to the notion of energy, and in *An Outline of Psycho-analysis* (1940a [1938]), he uses the expression, "the energy of the destructive instinct", in a way that implies the idea of degradation of energy.

In his 1915 paper, Freud (1915c) distinguishes between "self-preservative instincts" and "sexual instincts". Later, still adhering to a dualistic view, he introduced the hypothesis of "life" and "death" instincts. Freud was probably influenced here by Greek philosophy: he quotes Empedocles when discussing the classic polarization between love and hate. There are many other interesting dualities—for example, the distinction Thales makes between hot and cold. This is even more primitive and might evoke certain regressive aspects of the transference, between "hot and cold" or between "dry and wet", as in a new-born child.

In *Empédocle d'Agrigente*, Romain Rolland (1931) wrote of "original fissure in primeval chaos", to which I referred in my book on the psychotic experience (Resnik, 1986). Symmetrical pressure by two opposite forces transforms inert chaos into a vortex. I use the word "vortex" as a metaphor for the attempt to find a common language that will enable us to build our linguistic laboratory together.

To return to our clinical material: Liliane was telling me of her lack of energy, and at the same time of the great excitement she felt in her work environment: "I feel mentally destitute, yet I am never calm." Thinking back to the silence with which the session began, I realized how difficult it was for Liliane to tolerate pauses at the beginning of a session. "I am always excited. I cannot read quietly. I am not very easy-going nor accommodating." Here, Liliane showed her capacity for self-observation, projecting out of herself that part of her ego which is beginning to explore her mental space. "I am too demanding with myself", she went on, "too harsh, like my mother." Here, the idea of a superego figure comes into the transference, a mental image of an exacting maternal superego.

Freud wrote of the paternal superego, while Melanie Klein introduced the notion of the maternal superego, which emerges during the first year of childhood. The superego is so harsh during this first year because it is indissolubly linked to the death instinct. The baby has to get rid of this drive in order to live, because it is such a destructive agent, but in so doing, his environment becomes tinted with this destructive and persecutory intentionality; at the same time, the life instinct takes on all the aspects of a positive, syntonic and relational capability.

I ought at this point to distinguish between "destructive" and "aggressive". The verb "to aggress" suggests the idea of "going towards the other" [from the Latin *adgredior* (*ad* + *gradior*), meaning "to go into", "to go towards", "to go up to", "to approach"]. Freud at one point suggested that the death instinct contained the necessary degree of aggressive energy for development of the child's psychomotor aptitudes. In other words, as Melanie Klein was to point out, aggressive force, when combined with Eros, enables transformation of the destructive power of Thanatos into a constructive capability, "ad-gressive" energy prompting the individual to go towards the other. For Melanie Klein, the superego is not a static agent; it is a dynamic function with potential for development

"I often feel like my mother", said Liliane. "My mother has entered into me, and when I look in the mirror, it's her reflection I see in my face and in my movements." We have to admit that Liliane is no ordinary patient; she already has considerable "insight". What does Liliane mean when she says that when she looks in a mirror, she recognizes her mother's features? Which internalized maternal object takes hold of the microphone and speaks in place of Liliane? In the semiology of the transference, we must always be attentive to changes of voice and ask ourselves who really is speaking inside the patient, who is remaining silent and watching what is going on.

"I always have a photograph of my mother with me", added Liliane. "I have no particular love for her, but I can't help it, and I don't know why." After a pause—a pause for reflection, to my mind; there are pauses that are more like interruptions or breaks and others that are links and connections—Liliane added: "I read a book called *My Mother, My Self*, by an American writer [Friday, 1977]. When I was 15, I wanted to distance myself from my mother, to be a million light-years from her, to be on the other side of the world from her—but, in the end, I'm still there with her!" She was referring both to her internal image of her mother and to the photograph she had in her purse. "Maybe this is an identification?" she asked. I replied that I preferred not to answer that question as such, but encouraged her to think and talk about it. "I don't want be as harsh and as powerful as she is, but maybe I just have to be?"

She told me that her mother was very stern with her; this is Liliane's image of her mother. She added: "I had to become tough after my brother's death; he was four years old, and it was a very painful time." Liliane was eight years old when he died, and today it is as though she were dragging an emptiness along with her or inside her, a token of her dead brother. "I remember that my father cried, my mother didn't, and as for me, I just don't know. I cry sometimes, especially when I think of my old mother. I think I'm feeling less cold now." In the countertransference I could feel that her way of speaking was not as cold as it had been at the beginning of the session.

This takes me back to the matter of theoretical influences on Freud. He was undoubtedly inspired by Carnot's ideas on the transformation of kinetic energy into heat; this could be a useful metaphor for describing how drive energy can be transformed into warmth.

Liliane told me, a note of triumph in her voice, that she was able to cry; then she added, after a further pause: "My mother is obviously part of my life, and it's not easy to accept that! I would prefer to think of someone else—a man, for example." She went on: "My father was a relaxed sort of person. He would listen carefully to me, like you, but he was a bit selfish and didn't have much time for my mother." Here we can see an illustration of Freud's and Klein's theories about movement from maternal to paternal relationships. I have attempted to communicate as carefully and as exactly as possible what Liliane said and her associations.

What is the difference between psychic apparatus and mental space? Is there a specific locus in our body called "psychic apparatus", or does it permeate the whole body? Is there a locus or a "psychic apparatus" that we might call "mental space"? The question is one of possibilities, of hypotheses, of metaphors. I wonder, for example, what locus is involved when Liliane says: "My father didn't have much time for my mother." Was this a real event in her life? If so, at what age did it occur? Ten, fifteen? Did it happen in her parents' bed or in her mind—or was it actually taking place in that particular moment of the transference?

I suggested to her: "Your mother is isolated inside you, separated from your father." She answered: "I sometimes feel isolated inside, and often there is great confusion in me."

The theoretical notions of isolation and confusion are very important, to my way of thinking. In 1950 Herbert Rosenfeld wrote a key article on inner confusion in cases of chronic schizophrenia. For Rosenfeld, there comes a time in the therapy of the psychotic patient—or when the psychotic "nucleus" is reached in a neurotic patient— when the distinctions that enabled him to keep his objects separate weaken. When the long-separated internal father and mother come together for the first time, a state of confusion is triggered. (This is not the confusional state familiar to psychiatry, characterized by clouding of consciousness.)

In the following session, Liliane seemed more relaxed as she lay on the couch. After a pause, she said: "I'm trying to get organized." She touched her head as though trying to organize her thoughts. She went on: "In the last few days I have been feeling a little confused but at the same time different in my daily work. I think that the real danger is that my work could easily become a kind of drug. I'm clinging too much to work, putting everything I have into it—and I end up feeling empty." Later we shall come across other instances that will help us to understand what Liliane means by this "emptiness". She added: "What happens when I'm not working?"— then, as though answering her own question, "I don't know what to do with my time, it seems that I've got out of the habit of having any. Anyway I don't really know if there is a time–space inside me or not. Sometimes I fill it up, sometimes it vanishes. When I have time to myself, I don't know what to do."

Again the psychopathology of mental space.

It is worth remembering here that Liliane spoke of snippets from newspapers and magazines filling her mind. A psychotic patient of mine once said to me: "Why, when I see a car, do I have the sensation that there's a car in my mind? Why isn't it a mental picture?"

To be in touch with oneself—which is what we can expect from psychoanalytic treatment—means to be in contact with one's own affects and emotions. Emotion is movement, a flux of affects. This brings us once more to the duality in the pleasure–unpleasure principle, between life and death, corresponding to certain feelings and to the ability or inability to tolerate pleasure or pain. I use the word "pain" not "suffering", because they are quite distinct in etymology and in meaning. Suffering derives from the Latin *suffere* [*sub*: under; *ferre*: to carry], meaning "to undergo", "to endure", "to tolerate", "to allow". Pain derives from *poena*, "punishment", "pain", "torment". Some people are able to tolerate certain intensities of pain, others not, and medicine has taught us just how relative the notion of pain is. Some people who are very severely mentally ill—certain autistic patients, for example—feel no physical pain. A patient of mine had no need to go to the dentist, because he was able to auto-anaesthetize himself; it was only once his mental condition began to improve that he went to the dentist, because it was only then that he felt the pain of toothache.

To come back to the vicissitudes of mental space, we may wonder what Liliane meant when she said that sometimes she would fill up the time–space inside her, and at other moments this space would vanish. How can space vanish? I expect you have met people who give the impression of "flatness"; this may be their way of making mental space vanish.

I said to Liliane: "You find it difficult to tolerate space between things"—to my way of thinking, a pause is a space or gap between two presences. "That's right", answered Liliane. "I'm not sure I want to experience time as being something of my own. The shape of time is always changing—sometimes convulsed, accelerated, spasmodic." I had the impression at this point that Liliane was less on edge, and I added: "It's when there's movement that the shape of time changes." She nodded, saying: "Yes, movement saturated with anxiety."

She is experiencing suffering over her behaviour and anxiety about her body ego—the ego that emanates from the *persona* that is her body.

Liliane then became less anxious and added, touching her stomach: "I need peace. I have to calm my stomach, and also I must quieten my mind. But when I try to tranquillize my stomach, I eat too much, and I'd love to be slim! I suppose I work in the same way that I eat—to fill up an empty space." This is another way of filling mental space: by means of displacement, we can go from a space in the mind that is impossible to fill up to something much more concrete, and in so doing we experience the mental vacuum as a somatic void. If the emptiness in the stomach is not tolerated, bulimia will fill a mental vacuum that, thanks to displacement, is experienced as a somatic (body) phenomenon.

Liliane thought about this for a minute and then said: "Psycho-analysis is too deep", to which I added: "And you might fall down into the void." Liliane went on: "A bottomless pit is a terrifying thing."

Psychoanalysis is a way of observing the life we live, the external and internal worlds experienced as two forms of reality. It is not possible to argue for the idea of an internal world as part of our experience of body space, without the concept of a space for imagining, feeling, and thinking. Freud's notion of self-observation could be described as an eye with multiple vision, which, from the inside, can observe the external environment and, when

projected outside into the analyst's eye, can discover
internal perspective, volume, and substance. Magritte's
painting, *The false mirror* (FIGURE 1), representing an immense eye reflecting the sky, is a meaningful metaphor of
the ambiguity between body and universe, the dialectic
between internal and external world. Mirror reflection is
passive, dead, but a reflection in an eye penetrates inside;
inside the eye, an image takes shape.

Mental space without depth and volume is inconceivable; it requires three-dimensionality. The invention of
perspective in painting brought the notion of internal
perspective to art and architecture. When Paolo Uccello,
Filippo Brunelleschi, and Leon Battista Alberti refer to
perspective, the metaphor that comes to mind is that of a
space for thinking, a space inhabited by movement: the
emotion of the artist who, to quote Leonardo da Vinci,
"thinks with his hands".

The vertex (Bion) of what Alberti calls the visual pyramid is the focus of space and time and endows the
psychic reality of the world with an organized geometry; in
terms of the interiority of the individual, it corresponds to
the dis-covery of insight. In the analytic process, there is a
functional point or vertex, where the ego is temporarily
projected onto the eye of the analyst or out towards
some other locus in space and time and, through self-
observation or "in-look", discovers a bottomless void—a
chasm, which opens up to reveal an inner perspective
experienced as vertiginous anxiety by the patient. When
the self observes, it looks inside itself or appears at an
internal window, and in so doing risks losing its balance
and means of support. Insight, the capacity for internal
self-observation, may be experienced, as in Liliane's case,
as a terrifying bottomless pit. Marie Bonaparte wrote that
once when she was a young woman in Greece, she wanted

to swim in a place called "vortex". This was a black hole with a whirlpool, which could drag the swimmer to the bottom; local people called it the place where the waters are endless (Bonaparte, 1952). Before you can approach a whirlpool, you must be able to swim, and before you can explore a bottomless pit, you must be solidly anchored and securely held by the hand.

CHAPTER THREE

A space for dreaming

The theme of this chapter is the very complex and difficult question of dreams—a topic to which I have given considerable thought. Freud's "royal road" does, indeed, lead us towards the unconscious, but we must not forget that interpretation plays an important part also. Interpretation is mediation, an exchange network in which one party lends something to the other; this is the essence of transference.

My aim, as always, is to relate theory to clinical practice. Theorization of what is observed requires participation in a praxis where one is both actor and spectator in the given situation. Psychoanalysis is observation of both internal and external worlds—two forms of reality. As I said before, it is not possible to conceive of an internal world, part of our experience of our body and its space, without the notion of a space for imagining, feeling, and thinking.

From this summit we can look at reality in its double component of internal and external, as in another painting by Magritte, *Euclid's promenades* (FIGURE 2), where an easel–window draws us into playing with time and space, with internal and external reality; our perception is constantly in motion, we find ourselves continually in a state of emotion in the etymological sense of *e-movere,* with its connotation of movement.

Jeremy was a psychotic patient whose mental space was as flat as the surface of a screen. This phenomenon is not synonymous with psychosis; it can occur, for example, in schizoid patients. As I have already pointed out—and I return to this topic later, too—in certain pathological conditions in which mental space is deflated or flattened, there is no room for the three-dimensionality of the emotions; to create a space for feeling and thinking, for the emotions, requires so much effort that the resultant pain is unbearable. Sometimes one can feel empty, like the empty frame of a painting, as we can see in an untitled Magritte composition (FIGURE 3); or one may feel frame-less, perhaps searching desperately for a perimeter fence. Some patients seek refuge or frame in the mental space of the analyst, and the inexperienced analyst may seek his in academic theory, so as not to lose his way in the labyrinth of uncertainty.

The patient was lying silently on the couch; I, too, remained silent. The atmosphere became stuffier and stuffier—it was almost impossible to breathe. We could not move any more, we could not think any more. The atmosphere was becoming foggy; a toxic cloud—see Magritte's *The poison* (FIGURE 4)—that no one could control was permeating the entire session. After a long silence, he said, "I'm at home and I'm trying to frame some paintings for my new house. I feel a bit better now that I've said that." "That is exactly what we are here for together", I

replied; "to build a frame, to contain the bloating cloud
and try to make the air easier to breathe. . . ."

On this question of frame and content of psychoanalytic interpretation, the following passage from
Shakespeare's *Tempest* springs to mind:

> We are such stuff
> As dreams are made on, and our little life
> Is rounded with a sleep.
>   [*The Tempest*, Act IV, scene i, 148 ff.]

Here the frame that shapes the network of meanings is
sleep. The psychoanalytic session, too, may be punctu-
ated by sleepiness or reverie, an atmosphere in which the
developing exchange either becomes meaningful or consists of mere verbal sounds. The atmosphere we breathe
during a session is important; if it becomes impossible to
breathe, our task is to try to understand why we are on
the brink of suffocation. What is going on that cannot yet
be put into words or is already beyond words, what is
causing the feeling that everything is becoming paralysed,
thick, obscure, stagnant? There is an atmosphere which
envelops every session, just as the frame surrounds the
canvas, and the atmosphere itself may be the main chan-
nel for meaningfulness. It then becomes important to use
all one's sensory organs to capture the climate of the
relationship, the meaning adumbrated in the overhanging
clouds. This is particularly useful when there is the feeling of being dissociated, split off, separated from the
manifest content of what is being said. Communication
implies more than the act of saying words, it has to do also
with breathing, with presence. The session is a *Gestalt*—
an interplay between figure and background; sometimes
what appears incidental becomes the real focus of the
session, and what is said aloud is there merely to fill a
void. In analytic practice it is important to follow associa-

tions step by step, paying close attention to each new development; with experience, we learn that associations are not only spoken words or tones of voice, but also noises (internal, external), gestures, and acts.

A woman patient I was treating in London told me one day of her fear that a fire would break out in my consulting-room—there was a peculiar smell, she said. I stood up to make sure that everything was as it should be, and when I sat back down again, she said: "I'm glad I made you move." I felt playfulness in this remark—the patient was a schizophrenic who had spent many a long year in hospital, and it was only after two years of analysis that she had agreed to lie down on the couch. If we look at this episode in a metaphorical way, we could say that the image of a fire starting in the hearth is particularly apposite when it refers to the fantasy life of my patient, who had been so cold for such a long time; in psychotics, the change from the experience of time as frozen, paralysed, at a standstill, to one in which time is again in flux may occur quite unexpectedly. When one's world has been frozen, thawing out can be experienced as a catastrophe, a brutal transition from glaciation to conflagration. In making me move, the patient signified that the room itself had played a part in the dynamics of her associations; it was, perhaps, her way of saying that part of her internal space was becoming warmer.

Let us turn once more to dreams and to Liliane, the patient I spoke about in chapter two. Before I narrate one of her dreams, I will summarize part of the session that preceded the dream, because "setting" is a very ambiguous and at best relative concept, and I feel that, somewhat paradoxically, the associations concerning the dream begin before the dream itself and continue beyond it. In this session, Liliane said that she was less afraid to speak, and recently she had managed to travel by plane

FIGURE 1.   René Magritte, *The false mirror* (1928)
[see pp. 35, 52].

FIGURE 2. René Magritte, *Euclid's promenades* (1955) [see p. 38].

FIGURE 3.　René Magritte, untitled (1934)
[see pp. 38, 55].

FIGURE 4.   René Magritte, *The poison* (1939)
[see p. 38].

FIGURE 5.   Vincent Van Gogh, *The corridor of St Paul's hospital in St Rémy* (1889) [see p. 51].

FIGURE 6.   René Magritte, *Castle in the Pyrénées* (1959) [see p. 52].

FIGURE 7.   Odette's drawing: "the dog–bear dream"
[see p. 73].

FIGURE 8. Odette's drawing: "theatre, curtains drawn"
[see p. 75].

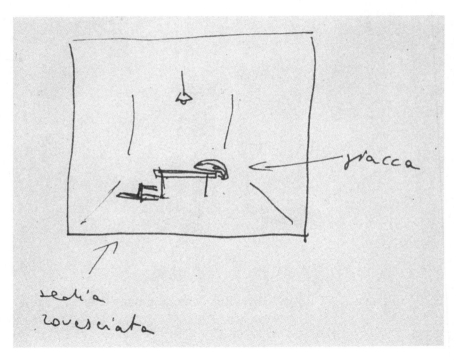

FIGURE 9. Odette's drawing: "stage" [see p. 75].

FIGURE 10.   Giorgio de Chirico, *Poet's pleasure* (1912–13)
[see p. 76].

FIGURE 11.　Giorgio de Chirico, *Autumn afternoon* (1920) [see p. 76].

FIGURE 12.   Giorgio de Chirico, *Mystery and melancholy of a street* (1914) [see p. 76].

FIGURE 13.   René Magritte, *Evening falls* (1964)
[see p. 81].

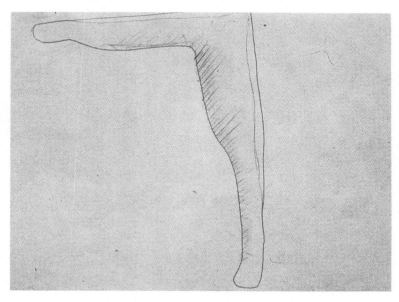

FIGURE 14.　Charles's drawing: "leg of table"
[see p. 81].

Figure 15.   Charles's drawing: "chair"
[see p. 82].

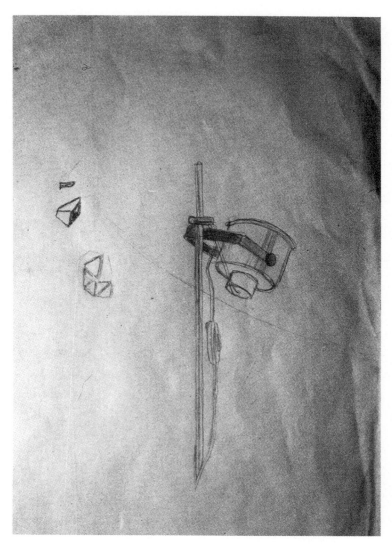

FIGURE 16.   Charles's drawing: "lamp"
[see p. 82].

FIGURE 17. Charles's drawing: "coconut shy" [see p. 83].

FIGURE 18. Charles's drawing: "car reversing into tree"
[see p. 84].

Fɪɢᴜʀᴇ 19.   Charles's drawing: "sailboat" [see p. 89].

Caballo de Troya

FIGURE 20.   Charles's drawing: "Trojan horse" [see p. 92].

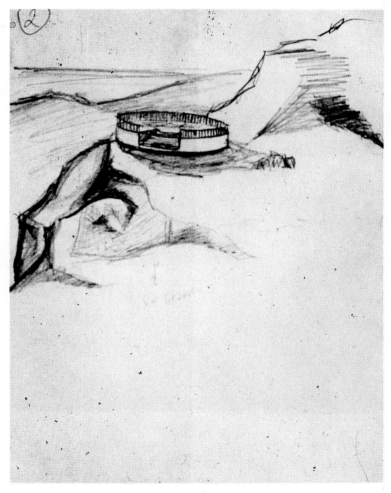

FIGURE 21. Charles's drawing: "landscape" [see p. 93].

FIGURE 22. Vincent Van Gogh, *Starry night* (1889) [see p. 96].

without anxiety. My impression was, indeed, that something was giving her inner support; I am convinced that her fear of swimming (and of being dragged down into the depths) or of flying had to do with her internalized mother or combined parental couple. We each of us have inside ourselves two parents who support us internally. In the Second World War, when Anna Freud was observing children in London during the Blitz, she remarked that those who had a satisfactory relationship with their family—in particular with the mother—were more able to stand the strain of the situation, as though they had inner means of support.

In Liliane's case, we must draw a distinction between the internalized mother who strengthens the ego and promotes internal consolidation (Winnicott), and the real, external mother. Even the use of the word "real" in this context is contingent, insofar as the external mother is always cathected with projections, so that perceptions are always tinged with fantasy projections. Psychotics, however, cannot acknowledge the intentionality of their projections; they are convinced that what they perceive is "real" and free of all fantasy content. For them, the world is a kind of anatomical back-cloth, with no element of fantasy.

Liliane was thus able to discover an internalized mother inside her mental space, thanks to the transference. We could also ask ourselves what our own projections are when one of our patients talks of his mother. This is a highly complex question; sometimes the danger is that we become accomplices of the imaginary parents. A vivid image of a persecutory mother could distort the analyst's role.

Every patient and every analyst comes to the session with his fantasies and his phantoms; these shadowy figures are the very matter of psychoanalysis.

Of her father, Liliane said: "My mother constantly invaded me, but at least she was present; my father was absent—for me, he didn't exist. It was much later that I discovered that he would talk things over with my mother and control the situation through her." Liliane associated her father, of whom she saw little in reality, with the fact that she cannot see me. Lying on the couch, a patient may have the feeling that the analyst has disappeared, and therefore want to look backwards in order to make sure he is still there. In Liliane's case, this may correspond in her internal reality to invisibility and condensation of the object, as in Lewis Carroll's Cheshire cat:

"Well! I've often seen a cat without a grin", thought Alice; "but a grin without a cat! It's the most curious thing I ever saw in all my life!" [*Alice's Adventures in Wonderland*]

Sometimes all that remains is a smile, a condensation in which everything is reduced to a single sign.

At one point Liliane announced: "I have a dream to tell you. *I was in the village where I was born. I was walking along the street near the market-place, holding a little girl by the hand. Suddenly, there appeared before me a woman with white hair, like yours, Doctor, pushing a little handcart with things inside it, salmon-coloured fabric. I had an argument with the woman, because she'd jostled us. I was indignant, and I threw all the textiles onto the roadway, stamping on the cloth and making it dirty. Who do you think that woman was? Pharaoh's wife in her chariot? The little girl who accompanied me was perhaps my sister or my daughter. There was a man with the woman, he asked us where we were going in such a hurry. I was going to the eye specialist's, but I'd made a mistake—I was, in fact, heading for the dentist's.*" Liliane associated the salmon colour to a similarly coloured carpet and to my first name: Salomon. I wasn't very pleased about that—I'd turned into something flat, a carpet . . . I was me and at the same time not me: I was also a pushcart containing an internalized object that Liliane had projected into me—a combination of maternal (my white hair was perhaps like her mother's) and paternal images.

My understanding of dreams is that the scenario, the narration of the drama of the dream, can never be exactly what has really been dreamt. In interpreting a dream what counts is the dream that is re-created when it is being narrated, for then all the feelings and perceptions arising from the session are brought together into play. The dream scenario as created during the session represented a street from her childhood: we had gone backwards, regressed, into another time—or Liliane had re-created another time in the present, re-actualizing it. The incident in the street did not have such weighty consequences as Oedipus's encounter with his father— an encounter that became calamitous because there was not enough room for both of them. The Oedipal situation was, however, present in Liliane's infantile ego part. My impression was that her adult ego was represented by herself, and the little girl was a playful ego; in her associations, she said to me: "When I was a little girl, I was like my daughter." I feel this is extremely important when looked at from the angle of the transference and its interpretation.

On this point, Rosenfeld, speaking of seriously ill patients who have lost all capacity for playful communication, stated that if we manage to re-awaken the child along with the adult ego, this will enable an infantile transference to develop (Rosenfeld, 1987). He meant the term to be taken in a positive sense, not merely as something regressive. Thereupon, he added, we can "get down

to work" precisely because it becomes possible to play—
each partner can bring along his playthings: the patient
his associations, the analyst his ideas and intuitions. It is
all this "recreative work" that makes it possible to invent
a new common language.

Liliane was setting the stage with, on the one hand, her
adult and infantile egos and, on the other, her internal
parental objects: mother and father saying to her, as it
were: "You should go to the eye specialist's because you
can't see where you're going." With these two aspects in
place, conflict became possible for Liliane in the maternal
and subsequently paternal transference, modulated by
her own history and with the analyst as actor.

She went on: "I can feel time getting mixed up." This is
an example of the phenomenon of illusion I pointed out in
Magritte's paintings. At one and the same time there is a
42-year-old patient and a 5-year-old child, plus the image
of the mother she will be for her daughter. This set of
different time sequences within the same space gives us
an idea of how condensation works in dreams.

"I didn't want to meet my mother here", said Liliane. I
added, "Nor your father, who noticed that you couldn't
see properly. There must be something very painful in all
this, because of the association to the dentist." "Now I
remember: I had a little plastic bag with me, and I didn't
like it." "You prefer fabric, it's less artificial. What do the
pieces of cloth make you think of, the ones the woman in
the dream is carrying?" "I think of good-quality old-style
fabric which has never been used, the kind grandmothers
keep stored away like relics. In fact, when I express myself
here, it's a way of washing my dirty linen in public."

I agreed with what she had said, and I emphasized
the fact that the textiles in the pushcart—fabric that
had never been used, good-quality cloth, still pristine—
were for her and for me. My understanding was that

the pushcart, personified by me in the session, in the sense of an object into which the maternal image could be deposited, represented my available mental space which Liliane was filling up with aspects of herself that she could not herself retain. Like a grandmother, she stored away her precious possessions in a trunk or a wardrobe; it was perhaps up to me to preserve and protect these treasures from her dirty attacks. Perhaps in her instinctual drives there was a blind, uncontrollable part for which she need an analyst/eye specialist.

Those were the fantasies I felt I could detect in the material, but we always have to remember (as Bion pointed out) that interpretations are no more than working hypotheses; if they prove relevant, the patient will respond, and the way is open for further associations. For example, in the case of a child who constantly repeats the same play sequence in his sessions, a good interpretation will open up further associations, and he will modify his play; this may indicate that a new transference space is unfolding.

After this exchange, Liliane remained silent—but this time it was a pause for thought. Then she went on: "I get into a black mood whenever I think of places I knew as a child, my home-town. I say I want to be rid of my mother, but she is always with me, in my bag. You must help me to put my thoughts in order." I replied, "Yet your textile has never been used and it's of fine quality."

"Yes, but what am I to do with it? Now, if I were younger. . . . Ah, I forgot, in another sequence of the dream *I give somebody the secret of eternal youth; the formula was kept in a silver sphere.* . . . Yesterday I saw a film about magic in Africa."

It seems obvious to me that Liliane wanted me to store inside my mental space the good-quality fabric she had never been able to use. Melanie Klein pointed out that it is sometimes impossible to integrate certain parts of the self, such as violently destructive or poisonous aspects, because of the risk of contaminating a pristine space (the good-quality fabric that had never been used). This is why patients sometimes need to project not only persecutory aspects, but also positive aspects if they are felt to be in danger. Pichon-Rivière (1952) examined this question in a paper in which he pointed out that in their interpersonal relationships psychotics get rid of their mad aspects either by making the other person insane or by projecting their persecutory aspects into the analyst or the whole institutional setting; this done, the patient then has to control the object in order to prevent re-introjection. This is why hospitalized patients so often wish to move to another institution: the one they are in has become contaminated—madness is always felt as coming from outside. The paper by Jorge Garcia Badaracco (1986) on "the maddening object" is also worth referring to on this point. When there is good-quality fabric—i.e. non-psychotic aspects—you need a mental space, a good safe-deposit in which to store this precious capital and prevent any risk of contamination. This helps us to understand better Liliane's feelings of guilt over the incident in the street: she has to protect the person who can contain, in his mental pushcart, the good-quality material that she has inside herself. In the dream narrative, Liliane attempts to get rid of the dirty aspects of herself. There is a question of identity here: she dislikes the plastic bag because it is artificial, and she would like to get in touch with the quality fabric inside her—her own true identity. "Doctor", she said, "I'm angry with myself. I don't like the way I am. I'd like to be authentic." Liliane was apparently reporting a dream, but I was aware that this was a colourful way of talking about the session.

Melanie Klein argued that the idea of depressive guilt is linked to accepting responsibility for one's own projections.

As Liliane spoke of her violent tendencies, she began to tug furiously at her clothing: "I need to tear something. When I became angry as a child, I used to tear my clothes; that excited me sexually. Do you think I'm mad, or that I need a strait-jacket? You know, I feel oppressed by my mother." The mother Liliane is speaking of here is obviously the internalized persecuting mother of the transference. I interpreted this to Liliane, pointing out that by getting forcibly inside me with her psychic merchandise, she wanted her analysis to begin for good now. She was using projective identification mechanisms to put inside me those aspects of herself she was unable to control or to protect, asking the analyst–mummy (and to some extent the analyst–daddy) to tidy all this up properly.

This could be seen as a kind of parasitic moment in the analysis. Each of us at the beginning of life goes through a parasitic phase, in which mother must do absolutely everything for us. This pattern of parasitic object relationships later becomes persecutory; Paula Heimann (1952) argued that when projective identification is too violent, sadistic, or destructive, feelings of claustrophobia or of persecution are aroused. The more violent the projections, the more the object into whom they have been deposited is felt to be persecutory—this could be the hospital, the bank, the analyst. The pushcart–mummy may turn into a prison and claustrophobic feelings are the consequence.

Liliane confirmed this, saying, "I feel so little, a prisoner in a cradle, or wrapped up in swaddling-clothes which stop me breathing." Again she felt the need to tear at her clothes, and became mentally aroused: "It's as though I wanted to get rid of my mother; I feel imprisoned inside my mother." In my view, the "clothing" Liliane would like to get rid of, above all, is her mother's womb, which at this point in time was not for her a protecting womb. Liliane, now adult, would like to force her way into the maternal space of the analyst, and the ferocity of her reaction is proportional to the violence of her projections. Liliane expressed in this way her sado-masochistic feelings in the negative transference, while at the same time indicating that she needed to tear at herself in order to open up some breathing-space.

Melanie Klein spoke of the fantasy of going back inside the mother's womb; in my experience this is, in fact, a response to claustrophobic anxiety. Birth implies coming out into the open; the human baby, unlike animals, is completely unprepared for leaving the womb's maternal envelope. If there are no welcoming arms, no good maternal atmosphere ready to hold him, birth is experienced as falling into the abyss. Melanie Klein put forward the idea of a very fragile primitive ego, which is too weak to tolerate the anxiety caused by the fantasy of being fragmented and lost in space. Since it cannot yet be unified, the ego needs a container; going from inside to outside is a catastrophic experience of fragmentation, of falling to bits.

When Liliane said she wanted to be rid of something, she added that she felt aggressive with respect to her sexuality. I think that attacking the womb represents what Ferenczi (1909) called "autoplastic identification": an object relationship is played out in a part of the mind with one's own body (or a part of the body, as in the example of Liliane's womb). Here, Liliane was representing her primary object relationship with the maternal womb.

The sample dream I have discussed with you shows how the dream material blends with different aspects of the session and elements of the transference. I have often wondered why Kleinian analysts do not publish their work on dreams; I think it must be because in their view dream analysis, like the rest, is one aspect of the analysis of the transference. There is a very specific quality to oneiric thought, which corresponds to the most embryonic messages the unconscious is trying to communicate. Dream analysis cannot be done in isolation, which is why I began by describing what had occurred before and after the dream itself.

In the case of psychotic patients, the problem is that oneiric messages and reality may become confused. They are unable to distinguish one from the other and have difficulty in realizing that dreams are a dramatic representation of something else. Bion said that psychotics cannot differentiate between dreams and reality; my own way of putting it would be to say that the psychotic is a dreamer who does not know he is dreaming. In order to narrate a dream, we must first wake up; waking up makes us aware that we have been dreaming, but the psychotic cannot come out of his dream.

There are, however, intermediate stages, nuances— for example, reverie, day-dreaming. . . . Eugène Bernard Leroy (1933), in his work on dreams and dreaming, included "waking day-dreams", together with the hypnagogic and hypnopompic images that precede and follow the actual period of sleep.

The dream as reported is not a facsimile of what the patient has actually dreamt; the story I tell myself about my patient is my dream. When I recapitulate a patient's clinical material, something of myself comes into play. I cannot correctly express what I feel without using the dream/drama, the word-games that are our mutual communication in my "laboratory". I know that when I relate Liliane's dream, I am also narrating my own, the salmon–Salomon dream. These transformations are part of the vicissitudes of that constantly changing laboratory that I call the psychoanalytic process.

CHAPTER FOUR

Mirrors, corridors, and tears

Having discussed the topic of dreams, we now turn our attention to oneiroid states, and from there to psychotic modes of thought; and I approach these subjects within the overall framework of mental space.

Dream time, time expressed as a spatial network, rhythm—these are the elements that compose the theatre in which dreams are enacted. Van Gogh's *The corridor of St Paul's hospital in St Rémy* (FIGURE 5), with its succession of spaces, gives us an idea of rhythm in space and the way in which space can be seen as an expression of temporality. This is the kind of time we encounter in dreams, or in certain places—Venice, for example, where my own dream-place is. When we visit a given locality at different times of the day, we see a different scene each time; this is scenery in motion, kaleidoscopic dynamics, where dream time is represented by a specific organization of space—Proustian space.

In chapter three I discussed Liliane's dream and the drama of the transference. Now I would like to turn to the oneiroid aspects of the transference, a topic that will bring me back to the idea of analytic space and setting. I will argue that three-dimensionality is a prerequisite for a space for thinking and feeling; in the psychotic experience the problem is the loss of depth or thickness through refusal of this space (and the resultant retreat into two-dimensionality).

Magritte's *The false mirror* (FIGURE 1) is a prime example of the dialectics of space: the image is so full of ambiguity that it is impossible to say whether we are looking at the sky situated inside the person or whether it is being reflected in the eye. In this dialectic we cannot legitimately talk of internal and external space, for each is a dynamic reflection of the other. One of my patients reported the following dream: *She was in the house she used to live in as a child when suddenly she noticed a ladder. She climbed down the ladder and went through a tunnel, which opened onto an outside area quite different from the one she knew in reality.* This image made her aware that insight, a journey into one's own internal world (self-knowledge), could help her to have a different perspective on the external world, which in this case was, in fact, much more colourful and lively.

In another Magritte painting, *Castle in the Pyrénées* (FIGURE 6), we see a rock in levitation. The rock is floating in mid-air, and on top of it stands a castle. This is an excellent illustration of what I am about to say concerning Irène, a 40-year-old patient of mine, neurotic and not psychotic. In one session, as she was lying on the couch, she hesitated a moment then said: "I feel empty", adding, "full of emptiness, there's such emptiness all around me."

Another pause, then: "The emptiness is getting thicker and thicker." In my countertransference, I could share this feeling; the atmosphere of the session was becoming stuffier and stuffier. "The emptiness", went on Irène, "is getting thicker still all around me; it's turning into a huge rock floating above my head. It's grey, and very heavy."

Irène had been in analysis with me for the previous four years. At first she was very inflexible. She told me that she had had a hard childhood, perhaps as hard as a rock, the rock she'd seen during this oneiroid episode. At present, Irène is a little less stony and more flexible, but at the same time more vulnerable; from time to time she still needs to harden herself and to protect herself with the kind of armour that Wilhelm Reich (1933) said was sometimes necessary to protect a very fragile ego. At other moments, her internal objects, as Melanie Klein put it, her internal *locii,* become as hard as stone and have to be ejected. Midway between dreaming and wakefulness, this experience could almost be called an optical illusion when looked at from the point of view of sensory perception. In fact, when Irène feels the atmosphere changing, this is projection—the hard, stony aspects of Irène herself—are expelled and turn into the huge rock, the "concrete" expression of the hardness inside her which she is unable either to contain or to tolerate. It is not a hallucination, but the underlying mechanisms are identical. In hallucinations, an internal sensori-perceptual experience of an internal object or object relation is projected outside by a sense organ (eyes, ears, nose, etc.). In Irène, the deep sense of conviction usually encountered in cases of real delusional hallucinations is missing. Irène began her session with a feeling of emptiness, and this "full of emptiness" became condensed and petrified.

This is an interesting example of an oneiroid experience in an analytic session, a day-dreaming in the transference. It illustrates the externalization of an internal situation that the mind finds it impossible to endure (the "magic eye" of the transference). The levitation, together with Irène's striving to give concrete form to a hard experience in her past and then push it away from her—all this indicates that she felt something in her life to be heavy and difficult to accept. We often describe depression and melancholia as a heavy burden; levitation, the fantasy of countering the pull of gravity, is an attempt to break free from everyday existence when reality—and the transference situation—is too painful. Irène was neither schizophrenic nor psychotic; she did, however, have a schizoid personality and could exhibit psychotic features. Schizophrenics often have the impression that their thoughts are floating in mid-air, as though levitating. Another patient told me that she had fallen into the sea; then, noticing that all around was blue, she decided that it was, in fact, the sky and not the sea. This countergravitational tendency is typical of the schizophrenic view of the world. Idealization is a form of projection that enables us to escape from everyday reality. De-pression is a "downward pressure", a fall; idealization is an "upward fall", as in manic states.

Let us return to what Irène was saying. "This feeling of having a rock hanging over my head is like a science-fiction film. . . ." She paused, then went on: "I feel I'm hanging in mid-air." Here we can see her identification with the rock floating in mid-air. There is a difficult and ambiguous point here, because it was for the moment unclear whether all this was happening inside her, in her internal word, or outside, in reality; this is often the problem with psychotics. "I'm moving away from the earth, but I love the earth; when I was a little girl, I used to like walking and running in my bare feet—but there were times when I wouldn't dare to, or my mother wouldn't allow me to." Irène was an only child, very close to her mother, to mother–earth, to her native village, to the countryside.

I have already mentioned the Magritte painting representing an empty frame (FIGURE 3). Maurice, a 42-year-old patient with a schizoid personality, often talked of his feeling of inner loneliness, emptiness, and what I would call "deflation". He would say: "When I feel lonely and apathetic, I'm unhappy." He is apathetic—i.e. without *pathos*, without emotion, lifeless. He went on: "And I'm afraid of feeling." After some six years of analysis, he was beginning to explore feelings, but he was afraid to get in touch with his mental space and with the feeling that he really existed; this was experienced by his fragile ego as too painful and distressing (mental pain). "When I'm not flat and insipid, I'm afraid to feel things. Sometimes I feel myself inflating to the point of bursting, or then again I feel like a clenched fist. It's as though I was trying to compress my inner space and prevent anything passing through." He made a gesture with his arm as he said this, then went on: "Sometimes I feel heavy when I don't succeed in compressing everything." Compress, oppress, depress, suppress—all end in the same suffix. "When I fail to compress everything, I feel sick. That disgusts me, I feel as though my stomach is full." (At one point Maurice had suffered from a gastric ulcer, which had since cleared up.)

This session must be looked at in terms of movement, because movement is what Maurice was talking about. "When my stomach feels full, I have the impression there's a foreign body inside me. If it doesn't melt, I have to throw it out, eject it." Is he speaking of an object? of a hole? One month before this session, Maurice had lost his father; he was, in fact, very depressed, sometimes with feelings that he was as yet unable to accept as his, sometimes in a cold, psychotic kind of depression. "I'm thinking of my dead father, I can see his cold corpse. When he was alive, he was often cold, distant, absent." A pause, then: "I see a blank space, unexpected, inside me. It makes me think of a night sky without stars. I feel flat again, turned into a strip of celluloid. I think I've lost my father." True psychotics are incapable of such nuances. One of my schizophrenic patients told me at the end of her analysis: "When I think of the delusions I had, I would say that my thinking had no subtlety to it, only unyielding dogma." I interpreted to Maurice that he had to be helped to deal with mourning and the loss of the object. What he was lacking inside was the internal presence of an absent father, a living memory, however distressing it might be. He felt deflated and needed this living presence to help him organize a space for himself to live in. An appropriate metaphor would be that of a house: how can we structure space inside if there are no columns or pillars—in other words, the phallic structuring function of a father? My term for the container–house plus central pillar is "structuring combined parents", as contrasted with the fantasy of "persecutory combined parents" described by Melanie Klein. The idea of good combined parents is present in Melanie Klein's work, though she did not formulate it explicitly, which is why I insist on this aspect too. A good internalization of maternal and paternal functions is extremely important, so that they can work together in the internal world: the one has a containing function, the other that of organization. Maurice said, "I'm afraid of suffering and of finding disorder inside myself, like a mental asylum."

Here the problem concerns the father and the organizing function: for Maurice, disorder means madness, and even when he communicates psychotic experience, he is not psychotic. "Sometimes I feel like a tailor's dummy, stuffed full of a kind of undifferentiated sawdust." The sawdust is homogeneous, there is no idea of difference or of otherness, but it enables Maurice to fill up a vacuum he finds intolerable. "Everything inside me is cold. I think of Prometheus, who had to steal fire because he felt cold. I feel I am an island, time is circular, sometimes it stands still, always the same." Though Maurice is not psychotic *stricto sensu*, we would call him borderline. He provides us with a good picture of stereotypes: a circular world, which, though it might be in motion, always remains the same (like the repetitive movements of autistic children), cold and lifeless. It is one way of pretending to exist— there is movement, but robotic and circular.

In another session, Maurice spoke of being inside a moving train; he himself was standing still, looking out of the window as the scenery flashed by. "The world is changing, but I stay the same. As I was coming to my session today, I noticed that the sky was blue, but there were clouds building up as though it were about to rain. Here on the couch I feel dry. From time to time I have the impression that tears will start to flow. . . . I'm thinking of my father." I pointed out that his internal sky was clouding over, he was ready to start crying. "But I don't know how to cry, crying would be a way of melting a frozen lump inside me." What Maurice was going through was extremely painful, but at the same time potentially invaluable. In my view, if someone can manage to communicate an aesthetic experience in such a manner, then a lot of work has been done by both parties.

Maurice went on: "I remember that my father never cried, he was as hard as stone; I can't cry either. I need to harden myself. I see myself in a dream without pictures, a cold, leaden dream. It's a corpse-like feeling, a dream of death." Maurice could not experience grief; in order to mourn, one must be alive. Freud, in *Mourning and Melan-*

cholia (1917e [1915]), puts it this way: "The shadow of the object fell upon the ego." Here, the shadow had become hard reality and took up so much space that Maurice felt absorbed into it, merged with this corpse he just could not get rid of. I felt, too, that the atmosphere of the session had become like a leaden dream, a hard, motionless reverie, a kind of annihilation whose purpose was to obviate any feeling of loss of the object.

I have given these two examples in the hope that the reader may sense that beyond the concepts of ego, ego mechanisms, object relations, defences, and resistance there is something immaterial in interpersonal contact: an atmosphere or, as I put it, an ecology of the encounter. It is in a certain type of climate that we introject and project; atmosphere is one element of the drama and plays a part in the semantics of it.

Still on the subject of *Mourning and Melancholia*, I would like to emphasize the difference between absence and void. The descriptions of mourning we find in Freud, Abraham, and Melanie Klein stress that the absence of the object leaves a void in the ego, together with a feeling of loss. With the help of a further example, I would like to demonstrate what this void corresponds to.

Some years ago, one of my patients, Mr Tavel, an intelligent man of 32, very inflexible and emotionally inhibited, with depressive tendencies, was having great difficulty in mourning the loss of his mother. He was well-adjusted and successful in his work—this is typical of the 35- to 40-year-old obsessional patient; nowadays the basic personality structure is more paranoid, perhaps because our culture has become more persecutory. Mr Tavel would frequently talk of his dead mother. She had died when he was 18, but it was impossible for him to mourn or even to express either his feelings of distress or his close emotional attachment; it was as though his space for thinking and feeling was sealed off. In his sessions he would continually come back to the topic of his mother and the emptiness her loss meant for him. One day he reported a dream: *It was his mother's funeral, but a very strange one, because everything ran in reverse. The whole funeral procession had to go to the cemetery to pick up the corpse and bring it back to the house. In the procession there was a priest and a rabbi* (whom he associated naturally enough to me). I knew that he had been unable to accept the loss of his mother when he was 18—he had not even been able to cry: his ego was too fragile to face up to such an experience. But as he was recounting his dream, I realized from the tone of his voice that he was feeling upset and was crying. At that point I made an interpretation: "When someone buries his mother, his ability to cry and to feel emotions, that part of his mind which is attached to his mother, gets buried with her." What I meant was that when there is loss of the object and depression, it is not only the object as such that is lost, but also a link, i.e. a part of the ego that is attached to the object. That part of the ego which is lost when the object disappears involves, as it were, a quantitative dimension. In Mr Tavel's case, he had lost a very large part; therefore, he could no longer "afford" to cry, because the amount of ego that remained was insufficient for feeling the loss of his mother. This was, of course, used unconsciously as a defence against suffering, but it also entailed much psychological impoverishment. That was why he needed the image of his mother and that part of himself still linked to her to be brought back to life and back into the house. The body is the self's "house"; if it is to be alive, it must be animated or re-animated. Mourning is always a double mourning: when someone we are attached to dies, something in ourselves dies too, hence the feeling of emptiness. When I said this to Mr

Tavel, his emotional response was intense, and he began to weep.

This was a crucial moment in Mr Tavel's analysis, a turning-point. From then on, he began to improve in the sense that feelings, emotional involvement with life, and the ability to feel pleasure made their entry into the transference, and therefore into life: emptiness, the void, became a place for absence. Mr Tavel said, "Now I feel permeable and alive." At that point we both recalled that at the beginning of his analysis, three years before, he would wear a raincoat to his appointments and keep it on throughout the session. Mr Tavel was to some extent justified in doing this, because he wanted to find out how permeable his analyst was and whether he could project things onto him. He was able to free himself from his raincoat once he felt he could trust me.

We could say that the shadow of the absent object returning to the house was a living shadow that contained traces of a large part of his ego. The work that mourning accomplishes is the restoration of an impoverished and mutilated ego; thereafter, the patient is no longer deflated, his internal world regains volume, a space in which the capacity for feeling and working through loss can find room.

Melanie Klein does not discuss emptiness to any great extent, but in her "A Contribution to the Theory of Intellectual Inhibition" (1931) she gives the example of a 7-year-old boy with obsessive traits who had a great desire for knowledge, for "intellectual nourishment". This reminds me of severely anorectic patients who do not eat food but never stop studying. Theirs is a kind of intellectual bulimia, the superficial function of which is a desire for knowledge, but which, in fact, is a way of filling up an empty space: cramming rather than creative knowledge. Melanie Klein's 7-year-old patient, too, had had feeding problems when he was a toddler; the feeling of emptiness in his body forced him to fill himself up with "knowledge–foodstuffs".

To return to the problem of mourning: the tendency to blank out feelings is typical of borderline and psychotic patients. It corresponds to turning the object loss that the ego is unable to tolerate into a void. Faced with death, the psychotic defence mechanism tends to empty the self of all feeling, thinking, and ability to experience loss; the therapeutic process has to retrace all these steps, transform the emptiness into absence, and encourage the process of mourning. This is what we saw in Mr Tavel's case. The work of analysis implies transforming emptiness and reviving painful emotions, while at the same time helping the patient to rediscover the pleasure of feeling he is alive.

Melanie Klein defined the paranoid–schizoid position in terms of ability to experience loss, i.e. the possibility of accepting the part as belonging to the whole. Differentiation is therefore a pattern for separation. To be able to experience weaning, or to go from one situation to another or one time to another, requires acceptance of the experience of death as intimately bound up with life. Going from the breast to spoon-feeding is also a fall into the depths of space, an internal depressive breakdown, a downward pressure, during which the infant requires a great deal of care and attention. Every parting, every shift in time is felt as another weaning. Birth is a kind of primary weaning; every subsequent transition implies facing up to loss. All cultures have their rites of passage at life's major cross-roads: birth, adolescence, marriage, death. As in every developmental process, the dialectic between death and rebirth is there to remind us that the new situation or developmental crisis is experienced as an abandonment, a feeling of total loss, collapse, death.

What, then, is this void, this vacuum, this emptiness? Einstein argued that it is a way of perceiving space, a property of space itself. I have already pointed out that the concept of vacuum changed in modern physics with the discovery of the electromagnetic field. When someone tells us he is empty, we should try to discover what he is empty of. Edwin Abbott, an English author who died in 1926, wrote a science-fiction novel called *Flatland* (1952), from which I have taken the following extract:

> Imagine a vast sheet of paper on which straight Lines, Triangles, Squares, Pentagons, Hexagons, and other figures, instead of remaining fixed in their places, move freely about. . . .

In this flat land, women are straight lines, soldiers and workmen are isosceles triangles, the middle class consists of equilateral triangles, gentlemen are squares or pentagons; the nobility have at least six sides—hexagons—but can have many more, at which point they receive the honourable title of Polygonal. Abbott tells us also of the Wisdom of the Circles (the priestly order and the highest class of all). Stereotyped movements, as those of the autistic child, could be thought of as circular: perhaps the impression of wisdom that emanates from the autistic child comes from the idea that a circle represents the utmost condensation of all experience. For Abbott, as for Lewis Carroll, the real question is one of knowledge.

In Euclidian geometry, we can measure distance and hence differentiate between *locii* that lie in the same plane, but we need post-Euclidian theory if we are to include the notion of a space for thinking, with its tri-dimensionality, depth, and volume. Bion was particularly interested in this topic.

I have already mentioned the importance of the concept of perspective and Leon Battista Alberti's visual pyramid, echoing Filippo Brunelleschi's optical pyramid.

The base is horizontal, and each line radiates towards the object. The eye of the responsive onlooker gives volume and depth to an otherwise flat plane as he comes closer to the object. My point is that the pyramid introduces the idea of perspective, the ability to see things from different angles, mental space as a container for life's experiences. This space for feeling and thinking is drawn directly from Freud's intuition of self-observation, the observing ego, the observing eye, which acquires inner perspective and gives space to and for the unconscious.

CHAPTER FIVE

Space, illusion, and hallucination

I would like to pursue my remarks on dream and dream-like thinking as opposed to thinking during waking hours—dream reality in contrast to everyday reality. We are able to narrate our dreams because we have the ability to differentiate oneiric thought from ordinary thinking. For the psychotic, on the other hand, this differentiation is blurred. In a psychotic crisis, the reality principle is dislodged, and an "unreality" principle takes over; hence the distressing un-reality concealed behind the psychotic's protective mask. Each of us deals with reality in his own way; the psychotic has to be inflexible because his ego is so fragile and unable to tolerate uncertainty. During this catastrophic experience, there is a crucial moment of painful lucidity, a watershed that concerns both his body and his mind—but the psychotic is unable to negotiate this decisive turning-point.

Psychosis implies loss of contact with reality, i.e. conflict with the reality principle and subjection to a principle
of un-reality or alternative-reality. The more fragile the
ego, as in the psychoses or severe obsessional neuroses,
the more thinking has to clothe itself in armour: a concrete, metallic, solid "principle". Since such patients tend
to feel fragmented in time and in space as though they
were falling to bits, defensive armour-plating is necessary
but not sufficient—their very thought processes must also
harden and solidify in order to be "convincing" and to
invade the reality of others. In a delusion, the objective is
not so much to maintain contact with the environment as
to convince and to impose another view of reality, coloured by persecutory projections. After the catastrophic
experience of a psychotic crisis, the debris of the breakdown seeks shelter somewhere in the environment: in a
tree or a rock or a river. When I talk of debris, I am
referring to the psychic apparatus. Bion (1957) showed
that one of the aspects of the psychotic experience of
reality is the development of aversion, a violent death-
wish directed against a reality principle that generates
doubt in the ego.

The narcissistic ego reacts violently against the outside world and its values, and even more violently against
the mind of the psychotic himself. The mind or psychic
apparatus is a mediator in our relationship with reality;
the dissociated psychotic ego attacks this apparatus,
which puts it in touch with unbearably painful situations.
Thereafter the scope of the attack widens, aiming now at
the Other's psychic apparatus—the analyst in the transference situation, for example. This projection is a kind
of induction, a co-presence, a hand-to-hand struggle, an
insidious atmosphere that makes it difficult for the
analyst to think. As the narcissistic ego turns away from

reality, the reality principle strives to maintain its superiority by decoding the external environment according to delusional criteria. The idea of delusional decoding is useful for understanding persecutory delusions and ideas of reference.

The Kleinian term "parts of the ego" is infelicitous in that it appears to imply a mechanical kind of disintegration of the ego, but it is nevertheless useful for understanding the fact that because of the reduced capacity for symbol formation in psychosis, reality is experienced concretely. We could suppose that in the psychotic crisis, the mind breaks down into both psychotic and non-psychotic parts. The psychotic approach is to deal with these fragmented bits and pieces in a "surgical" manner (Bion also speaks of the "cutting" attack that the schizophrenic makes on his psychic apparatus). In neurosis and psychosis (it is a matter of degree), there is flight from some aspects of reality, from relationships, or from anything that has emotional links to reality. For Freud, the distinction between neurosis and psychosis lies in the fact that the neurotic strives to maintain some kind of contact, however tenuous, with reality, whereas the psychotic alters reality so as to make it correspond to his own principle of reality/un-reality; delusion is an uneasy alchemy.

Odette was a young woman of 28 who lived with her family in a mansion house. One day she abruptly decided to leave her home-town and flee to Paris: she was trying to escape from crooks. According to Odette, her brother, a drug addict, had fallen into the clutches of a gang of criminals and drug dealers who supplied him with cocaine; as a result, he was going to squander the family fortune. She felt responsible for her family. In the months preceding our first meeting, Odette had become interested in everything that these criminals were up to, believing that their activities were designed, however remotely, to plunder the family wealth.

At our first appointment, I found myself in the presence of a slim young woman, very tense and unyielding, with an unblinking stare, which nevertheless from time to time would light up and become communicative. She looked unflinching, emotionally indifferent, and she had trouble expressing herself. In a cold tone of voice she described her delusion, which for her had the ring of absolute truth; this was why she felt she had no choice but to cut off all links with her family, at least for the moment, and seek medical help.

Her cry for help meant that at that point Odette was aware that she was unwell, or at least that she was afraid of going mad. In a perfectly intelligible and coherent manner, though cold and detached, she gave me to understand that everybody in her village knew the gang were out to seize her money: a boy singing in a neighbouring house had communicated in musical code the threats the persecutors addressed to her.

At one point in our conversation, I asked her whether she had dreams. Odette replied: "I thought—or perhaps it was a dream, I'm not sure—that *I was coming to your house, even though I wasn't familiar with it.* In this dream, or sort of dream, *you weren't at home, but you'd left a message asking me to repair your television set. I went to your apartment, it was on the second floor, and there was a very wide staircase leading up to your door. The door was open, and I was surprised to see that the flat was completely empty. When I went back down, I couldn't reach the street door, because at the bottom of the staircase a huge colony of centipedes was blocking the exit. The tangled heap of these insects formed a kind of spider's web that was impossible to cross over.*"

As Odette narrated what she called a "sort of dream", she remained immobile except for her hands, which began to move. Her actions were those of someone trying to escape from a trap he has fallen into. She looked at me carefully, in particular at my face and forehead, for a few moments, then added: "I would like to be a psychoanalyst." This was no surprise to me: I understood her to mean that she wanted to be inside my head, inside my skin, and to go up to the second floor, to see what it was like. I think this is quite legitimate, because when someone goes to a psychoanalyst, he cannot say what he has to say (consciously) until he has made sure he can trust the analyst; will this head be a good hospital, a good safe-deposit into which the patient can project the good parts of his ego he cannot himself hold on to? Because of his ontological insecurity, the psychotic (more than the neurotic) has to be an expert semiologist in order to decode the other person. Odette had to become my house and visit the different floors so as to know what would happen to whatever she gave to or deposited with me. The fact that, in the dream-story, the analytic place was empty meant for me that she had already put into my mental space, my head, her own feeling of emptiness. She had got rid of her persecutors—the centipede villains and their spider's web of complicity—on the staircase. Thus there are two levels, two degrees, two layers, two floors: Odette discards her persecutors "downstairs", and into my head, my mental space, my second floor, she puts her emptiness. The pathetic air she had about her, the *pathos* expressed as a painful but stereotyped grimace, gave me the impression that she had also got rid of fragmented bits of her mind, parts of her ego.

As I reflect on that first encounter, I think that Odette's need for help, for reparation, and her feeling that she was a broken-down piece of machinery had been projected into me by means of the pathological mechanism we call "projective identification". Herbert Rosenfeld pointed out that one of the characteristics of psychosis was to occupy the analyst's space and to merge with the analyst by means of the array of defence mechanisms psychotics can call upon (Rosenfeld, 1987). I have observed that the psychotic is also keenly aware of the danger of "trans-fusion"—i.e. the confusion between one's own space and that of others. Given his fear of losing his own boundaries and becoming confused, the psychotic tends to withdraw autistically or remain spatially remote and use mediators in order to communicate indirectly. It is precisely for this reason that when a psychotic is in analysis, the question of contacts with the family becomes so acute. Kleinian analysts tend to avoid diluting the transference in this way with family members. However, psychotic patients, like children, do not come alone to their sessions; further, the friend or relative is often transporting some of the patients' messages. Nowadays, it is commonplace to state that psychotics, like drug-addicts and borderline patients, cannot contain their shattered ego; they live fragmented in their families. Bion called this "being too sociable" in the sense that there is too much externalization. I have often thought that autistic mannerisms may be ways of mimicking movements of water, wind, or other natural elements. Nature becomes alive, for that is where fragments of the psychotic crisis hide in order to lose their more human aspects: identification with an inanimate object is one way of transforming reality, one's self or one's mind, into something that is divested of emotion.

The fact that Odette had to repair my television set is, of course, role reversal: she is my therapist, having deposited her illness in my head together with her disturbed, mechanical, fragmented ways, in an attempt to free herself from her role as patient. Being a patient is a terrible wound for the narcissistic personality; such patients have to find another level of thinking or deluding reality or another object—the analyst or some other person, or thing.

In another session, Odette began to fear that she might not know what the analyst was thinking and hence that she would no longer be in control. She emerged from her indifference to say, "In a way, the crooks and the spider's web are here." I replied, "I'm not sure, but perhaps the crowd of centipedes managed to come into the session and change the way things used to be. Your environment has been modified."

These are hypotheses, as all interpretations are. Only the development of the transference will tell us if they are relevant. The patient with paranoid delusions tends to interpret everything in his environment as having special reference to himself; here I was saying to Odette that perhaps there was some kind of misunderstanding and that the centipede web that had invaded the session had mixed up our roles, so that we no longer knew who was patient and who analyst. The confusing, enveloping, Kafkaesque web reminded me of what Bion called "engulfing and encysting the object", referring to projective identification, which, like the spider's web or the retarius's net, entraps and immobilizes the object. In the session, Odette was able to create an atmosphere for enveloping the analyst and so take possession of him.

For the next six months, Odette came daily to her sessions and remained highly motivated. We made progress in analysing the psychotic and neurotic aspects of the transference, and this enabled us to free ourselves from the persecutory web. Communication became freer and more lively, with feelings and emotionality. The delusional aspects continued for some time, but their theme changed from criminal *mores* to politics. Every colour that she noticed in the street, in her flat, or in my consulting-room was the mark of some political allegiance or other: red represented communism, white conservatism, and black was the diabolic side of every belief.

One day, as she was out walking, Odette saw children coming out of a school. This pleased her at first, but then she had the impression that they turned into puppets and dolls. She herself, though adult, felt she had an infantile ego, inhibited and unable to play. "When I was a girl, I never used to play much", she said. Melanie Klein pointed out that the inability to play in a child is a symptom of serious disturbance. Odette went on: "When I saw the children come out of school today, I felt inflated, as though I were pregnant." She paused a moment, then: "I'm interested in philosophy" (she had been a philosophy student but had abandoned her studies) "and the word which comes into my mind is 'maieutics'." "That might mean letting ideas be born, don't you think?" I said. Odette added, "I'm thinking of Socrates' mother; she was a midwife." I interpreted to her that I was to be a wise midwife [midwife in French is *sage-femme*—literally, "wise woman"] and understand that she needed help in setting free the child inside her, who until now had been immobile, inhibited, lifeless, like a puppet or a doll.

Odette interrupted her analysis after about six months and went back to her home town. She felt much better, but though she was less persecuted, she was not by any means cured. Two years later, she phoned me to ask me to help her again. Something very serious had happened: her brother, the drug addict, to whom she felt very close, had died of an overdose. Her fantasy about being pregnant had become reality: she now had a beautiful daughter, who was coming along fine. Odette, however, was finding it difficult to communicate with her; also, she was afraid her baby might fall ill if she herself was not cured. She had tried to take up her studies again, but she did not feel capable of thinking and studying; she wanted me to help her give birth to her ideas and to take care of herself. After her brother's death, the feeling that the world was threatening had once again come to the fore.

Odette was better than when I had first met her, but she still tended to become alienated from and lose contact with reality. She reported a dream: "*I can see a soft toy, it's a big black dog or a kind of bear. It's as big as I am, and it's crying. The strange thing is that its tears are cube-shaped and ice-cold, like very dangerous ice cubes that could engulf and entrap anybody who comes too close. I was afraid to approach it.*" She hesitated a moment, then continued: "I feel so little. . . . Could I draw my dream for you?" Her drawing (FIGURE 7) is remarkable. The dog–bear has a pathetic expression, a latent *pathos,* hinting at immense distress. It made me think of a reified double. I asked her what she thought of her drawing. "The eyes stare emptily, the hands are cut off; I think of my brother with his hands tied, a prisoner of his addiction, and now he has departed from this world. I feel limp." I commented, "Limp like a soft toy dog? It must be distressing for you not to be able to cry feelingly over your brother's death. And it must be painful also not to be able to respond to your daughter with sufficient emotion, or to feel that you are a puppet, a soft toy that can't express pain and grief. The ice-cube tears show how much you need to cry, and also the difficulty you have in accepting your emotions and your warmth." I think that the cube shape refers also to an inflexible, stubborn, implacable part of her personality.

Odette went on, "I feel weak, empty inside. . . . I can't feel anything, except for this sensation of being full up."

I reminded her that before she had interrupted the analysis, she had told me of children running out of school
and turning into puppets, mechanical beings. Odette
then spoke of colours again, saying that my pullover was
warmly coloured. I had the impression that she realized,
by contrast, that the coldness was inside her, her warm
aspects having been projected onto my pullover as onto a
screen. "I feel a kind of anxiety in my stomach, a fear or
a hole. My brother's death has left a huge hole inside me."
When it is impossible to accept the death of someone, we
feel we have been robbed of all emotion; the emptiness,
the void becomes firmly entrenched. If, in turn, this
emptiness is unbearable, we try to evacuate it from the
mind; by dissociating *psyche* from *soma*, we locate it
somewhere in the body—for example, the stomach. This
is the pattern for hypochondriasis.

In another session, Odette looked at the white-
coloured curtains in my consulting-room and declared: "I
feel as flat as those curtains. . . . Inside my head there's a
piece of white cloth just like those curtains. My life is
cold, deflated." I interpreted that the place for thinking
and creating images, her head, was like a screen, a piece
of cloth: lifeless. "I think of all the people who are dead:
my brother, a friend of the family. . . . I feel dead too. I
have a headache." "It's very distressing to feel dead–alive",
I replied. Feeling dead and having a headache at the same
time means that on a somatic level Odette was aware of
the distress that being simultaneously dead and alive
caused in her. Here again mental pain is displaced in
order to avoid recognizing it as such.

Then Odette glanced at a chair standing near the
window, a look of terror on her face. I have on other
occasions spoken of this chair, with respect to which
many of my patients develop transference. There is a
hand-crafted pattern on the chair, which Odette inter-

preted as "the chair's thoughts". Psychotic patients often make contact with the inanimate objects that are part of my working environment rather than directly with me. Odette continued: "I see someone sitting in that chair, one of my brother's girl-friends; I don't like her, she had links with the underworld."

In the following session, Odette looked at my bookshelves and noticed a book on the theatre. "I'm thinking of the theatre", she said. "My brother wanted to be an actor or a director." "Theatre is not the same thing as the cinema or a screen; it isn't flat", I said. Odette went on: "I can see a shape with the curtains drawn, making a kind of screen (FIGURE 8). And now the curtains open, I can see the stage; it's empty except for an upturned chair and a table. The only person in the play has left the stage, forgetting his cloak on the table" (FIGURE 9). This is an obvious allusion to the end of a session: when Odette leaves the stage, she leaves something of herself behind. She quits the transference stage, terrified at finding within herself a space for being alive, for feeling, for thinking. Accepting the suffering caused by the loss of a loved object indistinct from a part of herself produces an experience of mental pain as a precondition for coming alive. The indissolubility of her union with her brother, like her feminine ego undifferentiated from her masculine ego, is difficult to grasp clearly, but the cloak may represent Odette and the object in confusion, or her bisexuality; she had abandoned it in her rush to escape from a stage scene that was about to open onto potential suffering. In this session a new dimension was opening up: the possible transition from flatness to the third dimension of depth and volume. It is difficult to convey the atmosphere of the session, the air we were breathing, the movement, the question of whether there was a human being there or a puppet. Perhaps Odette was dissociated—i.e. she had emptied her own cloak of all living force; her real psychotic existence was taking place outside, in the street, on another planet, or in another galaxy—somewhere in a wandering, fantastic world. This is the atmosphere we feel in some of de Chirico's strange empty townscapes of Ferrara, where immobility reigns, nothing moves (Figures 10 and 11)—but then again, sometimes a child runs into the light (Figure 12), an infantile ego part that has not forgotten how to play and can set in motion the possibility of a responsive and living transference with the analyst.

CHAPTER SIX

A geometry of space: mental space and the transference

To illustrate what I have to say about the geometry of mental space, I will take the example of Charles, a 22-year-old schizophrenic; he is of Spanish descent and has been in analysis with me for the past two years.

He came to his first appointment accompanied by his mother and father, and we all sat down in my library. Charles struck me as a slim, handsome young man, but tense, silent, indifferent to his surroundings, locked up in his isolation. His mother told me the history of his illness. Charles had become more and more withdrawn during the previous three years and had interrupted his studies at the Madrid Academy of Fine Art. The family had moved to Paris and intended to settle there for the following few years, at least. Charles's regression worsened: he had become like a little boy, unable to leave his mother. He would follow her everywhere, repeating her movements

77

like a shadow. His only contact with the external world was his computer. Given his devitalized robot-like appearance, it was easy to imagine that this computer represented a mirror-image of this young man. Charles would spend hours at the keyboard, and when the computer was unable to answer the questions he typed in, he would become furiously violent and impulsively aggressive; perhaps he felt despair at his inability to sustain some kind of dialogue with this inanimate double, which, in his way, he was trying to make human. He would lash out at it—so much so, in fact, that on one occasion he completely destroyed it. This meant even greater isolation for him, a cold depression, i.e. without emotion or internal movement.

While his parents were telling me all this, Charles was staring at one corner of the room. In terms of mental space and the transference, I would say he was transferring something from inside himself to this corner; in other words, Charles did not establish a direct transference with me, but we met, as it were, indirectly, in the corner of the room. He glanced at me, then immediately looked towards the corner. I had the feeling that with his eyes–mouth he had first incorporated me inside his space, then deposited me into the corner of the room. The omnipotence of schizophrenic patients, as in certain obsessional neurotics with pronounced narcissistic traits, is expressed more in terms of a struggle for control of the time and space of the analysis rather than as outright hostility towards the rules of analysis or the transference situation. Because of their feeling of insecurity, they want to be the stage managers of the analytic situation.

While I was having these sensory infra-verbal impressions, the mother was talking about Charles, the removal to Paris, and their new home. There is a servant's room in the flat, and the parents had thought that Charles could use it as his den. He was very clever with his hands, he could manufacture objects and restore antiques. This was Charles's way of expressing his desire to be cured, and also his wish to be his own therapist: he was the one who would repair the object.

At that moment I had the impression, as we looked simultaneously towards the corner of the room, that we were making contact with each other; it was almost as though we had arranged to meet in that particular spot. I formulated my first interpretation, saying to Charles that I felt he was looking for a place in which he could feel protected, so that he might get back in touch with himself. I had the impression that he was somewhere else, not "in" his body: his psychic ego, alienated from his body ego, had become settled in another body, or in some geometrical location, and as a result his own body had become empty. I was trying to meet him somewhere in the corner. Charles responded to my hypothesis by giving me a rather more lively look than before. The first words he uttered were "servant's room", which I took to be an allusion to something that would be of service to him in the room where we were sitting.

At the end of this first meeting, we tried to draw up a preliminary contract for the analysis. This was extremely arduous, for Charles did not live within himself, but to a considerable degree elsewhere—inside his mother, or in other locations. This is the major problem in psychosis. I offered to take Charles in analysis, with four sessions per week.

Charles came alone to his first session. He was still silent, speechless, and once again I realized that he would speak through his eyes: he looked all around, at everything, using his eyes in a "tactile" way, as Henri Wallon put it. It was his way of feeling things: touching books or paintings. I asked him what he was looking for, if there

was something he was interested in. "History", he replied.
"What history?" I asked. After a short pause, he answered:
"In Spain, there was Charles I, then Charles II, Charles III,
and Charles IV. There was disagreement between them." I
had the impression that time had come to a standstill and
had taken on a spatial dimension; he was reciting the
historical sequence of the successive Charleses as though
they had existed concurrently. I remarked that each of
them had settled in his own kingdom, and they found it
difficult to talk to each other. Charles answered: "Yes, if
one of them speaks, it means war", adding: "It was only
when Charles V of Austria came along that there was
reconciliation, and the kingdom was united."

This was Charles's way of telling me that there
were four Charleses inside him, each omnipotent and in
disagreement with his fellows. This is an excellent description of schizophrenia, which before Bleuler used to
be thought of as *folie discordante* (Chaslin, 1920). I said
to Charles that he was worried about agreement and dialogue between these different parts of himself and that he
needed someone like Charles V (I didn't say King Solo-
mon!) to unite his kingdom, his ego. I added, "I am not
Charles V, but perhaps the two of us working together
may be able to do some uniting."

A silence followed, during which Charles seemed to be
thinking (perhaps the ideas floating in the corner of the
room had returned to his mental space). He touched his
nose and said: "I caught a cold, I have a runny nose." He
glanced at a book, then at another: looking at something
was his way of making contact with my thoughts transformed into an object—my library. He stared intently at a
book on mental health, and after a pause said: "It's hard."
All this seemed quite coherent to me: it was very hard for
me, but even more so for him. I commented: "You feel you
need to harden yourself, to put on armour. If it cracks

open, the hardness could melt, and everything would run out of your nose."

Many years of experience with body fantasies have taught me this way of attempting to put someone in contact with himself and—even more difficult—with someone he is unfamiliar with. I represented for Charles something uncanny. He was quite justified in trying to touch all the thoughts he felt were surrounding him; in this way he could know what I was thinking and whether there would be a place where he could think about himself.

Another pause, then Charles went on: "I'm thinking of someone who's violent and at the same time likeable." My idea was that two contrary instinctual drive aspects of Charles were trying to make contact. "I'm thinking of a broken guitar", he added. That reminded me of another Magritte painting, *Evening falls*, where the window marking the boundary between interior and exterior has a broken pane (FIGURE 13). I commented: "Inside your armour-plating there is somebody who feels broken (the guitar that needs repairing) and has to be helped back into harmony, back into equilibrium. But at the same time he is afraid his violent aspect could cause damage—it had already destroyed his instrument for reverberation and communication, his mind." Charles replied: "There are things in my head that are absolutely impossible to communicate. Ideas may change into shapes, figures, or even into nothing at all."

In the following session, after a moment or two of silence, Charles turned his head towards the white curtain on the window. I asked him if he could see anything, and he answered: "Yes, the leg of a hen." Using the implements at our disposal, I asked Charles to draw the leg of this hen. In fact, what he drew was the leg of a table (FIGURE 14); I pointed this out to him. His mother had told me that when they moved into their new home in Paris,

Charles had found a table in a rubbish dump and had repaired it.

Shortly after this, Charles's eyes moved to the chair standing next to the curtain. He wanted to draw it. He made an excellent and highly detailed sketch of the chair, except for the fact that it had only one leg (FIGURE 15). So, now we had a table-leg without a table, and a chair with only one leg. On a theoretical level, we could ask ourselves whether these are part-objects or fragments of objects.

Charles studied the chair with considerable interest and made comments that seemed to me to be full of wisdom: "The chair is very useful for dispersion." I took this to mean that at that particular moment the chair could give refuge to his feeling of being fragmented. Then he looked at the pattern on the chair—hieroglyphics would be an appropriate word to describe it—and seemed fascinated by the language of the chair. He was experimenting with hermeneutics, trying to decipher the object. "It's probably filigree, there's a kind of logic to the writing." In his reified state, Charles had put himself and all his fragments into this unfinished chair, as incomplete as he felt himself to be at that point, with no leg to stand on—floating in mid-air among the clouds. I thought it was quite logical for some of his wandering ideas to settle into his own "house for living in"—i.e. his body and his mind. I pointed out to him that in his drawing the chair did not have its full quota of legs, one of which seemed to be in the previous sketch he had made.

Charles glanced at my lamp and decided to draw it; in fact, he drew only part of the lamp (FIGURE 16). I felt this to mean that he could perceive only a small part of reality, and also that there was a little glimmer of light in his world, which could be projected onto a real object. The anatomy of a landscape meets the physiology of the eye with which we look at it; we breathe life into it with our thinking. Man is a maker of fantasies; it is they that enliven reality and make the environment meaningful. In the fragmentation of a psychotic crisis, reality explodes. Charles was showing me both the fragments and his attempts to live together in the same space with those he had projected into my furniture and my space. What he feels to be parts of my personal inner space was making contact with the fragments that remain inside him after the catastrophe.

Now back to the session itself. After another pause, Charles wanted to do another drawing: a rough sketch of a funfair coconut shy, with a middle-aged man taking aim. Beside this is a miserable-looking tree, which could almost represent someone raising his hands as though to implore help; there is also the idea of carrying a heavy burden (FIGURE 17). This was Charles's way of expressing his need for help and his feeling of heaviness, a typical feature of melancholia; such patients carry a heavy weight on their shoulders, an accumulation of things they find unbearable.

Charles glanced at me as he was making the sketch; I returned his look, with the impression that each of us was trying with his eyes to touch the centre of the other's target. There was a moment of tension—perhaps anxiety resulting from what I had said or had touched in him previously—then Charles relaxed and smiled.

In the following session, Charles recounted some childhood memories; something was beginning to open up ever so slightly. When he was 7, he had lived in Central America (the father travelled a great deal), in a big house. One day he had the feeling that there was an intruder in the garage, and he had told his mother so persuasively that she had called the police. In fact, it was the head of a statue, standing back in the shadows, a sculpture of one of his sisters.

Whenever he felt cold or afraid, Charles would try to get close to his younger sister, with whom he had a highly eroticized relationship. When he was a little boy, he liked to sleep in her bed; this brings to mind the corner of the room he would stare at—perhaps it meant something warm and exciting for Charles. My hypothesis was that Charles took great pleasure in being drawn to a corner that warmed him up, contained him, breathed life into him—this may be why he would search for his sister's crotch, the angle–corner between her legs. His mother had several times seen him try to approach her and touch her between the thighs. When I mentioned to him that perhaps he was seeking warmth and comfort, he replied, "I find angles very interesting, I'm interested in geometry." I went on, "Yes, but a living geometry", since he had obviously construed my interpretation in terms of Euclidian, plane geometry. Perhaps what his mother had said was experienced by Charles as persecutory.

Charles often spoke about lakes and a house that had been destroyed—a house with marshlands all around it. To me, this meant a place where it was impossible to find a solid footing; hence his feeling that it was difficult to stand on his own feet and be himself. He was an empty house that had been razed to the ground, about to be engulfed in the shifting sands of the earth–mouth, chaos.

At another moment, Charles drew a car reversing into and colliding with a tree (FIGURE 18). It was his mother's car, which he had taken, and he had had an accident. According to his mother, this corresponded to the time when Charles had begun to withdraw from the outside world, when he had first begun to feel different and fragmented. Getting into the mother's car or into the sister who closely resembled their mother, his little mummy, implies in my view pathological projective identification. It is a manifestation of severe agoraphobia, the dramatic inability to deal with open spaces, hence the need always to inhabit someone else's body. In the transference we meet this kind of phenomenon when someone "gets stuck into us". Charles gets into the car body, into his sister's crotch, into his mother's or his sister's clothes. He remembered how, as a young boy, he liked to dress up in his sister's dancing costume; we could think of this as his need to find a space for himself inside his sister's clothes–being.

Each of us has to find a common language that will act as a mediator between two different worlds—a means of communication that will help each of us not to feel obliged to enter into the other's "bodywork", as Charles seemed to have to do. This problem occurs frequently when we discuss clinical material: when I report a patient's dream, it is to some extent my own dream that I am narrating. In other words, when I talk of Charles, I am, in fact, giving my version of what happened, and I have to accept responsibility for it with all the imperfections and imprecision that that might imply. Given that, I can then put you in touch with things that are difficult to communicate and open up another space for thought and discussion. I have already stated that I prefer the term "double transference" to transference and countertransference; if we place ourselves in a transference situation, neurotic or psychotic, without losing our boundaries, then we will learn much from our patients. The patient tries to enter into the analyst, not only with the ill aspects, but also with the healthy parts of his personality, which he finds impossible to protect. Sometimes the psychoanalyst divests himself of part of his therapeutic role and projects it into the patient; in this way, as Searles (1979) points out, the patient can take on the therapeutic role. I think that what is important in psychoanalysis is not the obvious, but questioning the obvious. In Joyce McDougall's (1978) words: "Being an analyst means letting oneself be called in question by the patient and to call oneself in question." This is the meaning of the term "working through"—working through space, working with the space that opens up the possibility of dialogue. For there to be communication and dialogue there has to be separation; this is the problem encountered by those who do not manage to climb out of the bodywork, to come out of their space.

CHAPTER SEVEN

A space for delusion,
a space for creation

I n chapter six I described the case of Charles, a young man who suffered from a schizophrenic disorder, about the vagaries of my sessions with him, and about the birth and development of the transference. Charles had constructed a geometrical kind of thinking in the transference: he would glance towards a corner of the consulting-room, indicating that I should look in the same direction—towards the place where we had arranged, as it were, to meet for that particular session.

Charles was remarkably good at expressing himself figuratively. I mentioned that in his third or fourth session he had drawn a middle-aged man standing at a funfair stall, with a tree close by; this represented, in my view, the moment when our eyes—the patient's and mine—were about to meet. When I began talking, Charles looked at me as though he were trying to look inside, towards the centre. This was also how I would look at him occasionally, so it was a kind of mutual exploration. Given his ontological insecurity and the fact that I was only just getting to know him, this was a perfectly logical state of affairs. I interpreted the tree as perhaps implying that he needed help, but also as representing the heavy burden he had to carry.

I also narrated an episode that had occurred during the summer holiday just before he fell ill, when he had borrowed his mother's car and reversed it into a tree. In the current session, I pointed out the link between this and the tree Charles had drawn: the tree had withstood the impact, and perhaps in the transference Charles was beginning to find something supportive. Symbolic-ally, this could be represented as a crash, an accident, a traumatic incident, which, as Freud put it, is not so much the cause as a precipitating factor, producing regression and re-actualization of a psychotic or neurotic pattern of response. As Charles was recounting this incident–accident, I had the almost physical impression of being touched; sitting behind him in the session, I was turning into the tree he had driven into with such uncontrollable anger.

I hinted, too, at the difficulty psychotic patients have with their "being-in-the-world" and with other people—a difficulty that induces "athletic" defence mechanisms in order to leap through space and time and into the Other: in this case, the analyst. In the case of Charles, getting into his mother's car and trying to get inside me are typical examples of a psychotic object relation. Being inside rather than with the Other, projecting oneself forcibly into the mother–car or the father–tree or into me in the transference, is typical of pathological projective identification.

This type of projection serves less to communicate than to explore and, in the final analysis, to invade. The psychotic patient, or the psychotic part of the ego, abandons ship, turns away from its own body in order to take possession of and settle down inside someone else.

Abandoning a sinking ship corresponds to the catastrophic crisis that, Karl Jaspers argued, was a feature of schizophrenic experience. This fantasy was expressed in another drawing Charles made: he drew a boat, and he sketched himself hidden behind the sail (FIGURE 19). Charles had set sail in an analytic craft in which, for the moment, he would be happy just to float, but he hid himself away—quite rightly, too, I think, given the threats that day-to-day living meant for him. Being inside the Other, inside his body or his mental space, is a sort of physical or mental counterfeiting or plagiarism—the kind of situation when, for example, somebody dresses up in someone else's ideas. For an analyst, this is, as it were, a rite of passage; but the patient will have to ask himself how he can get back inside himself and put his own clothes back on. We may recall that as a child Charles liked to dress up in his younger sister's dancing outfit. Sometimes he enters into the object and finds himself locked in and imprisoned. In the transference, for example, he gets inside my head and puts on my ideas, my psychoanalytic clothes: he does this at home and in the hospital, where the other patients take him for a psycho-analyst (or so he tells me), and in my consulting-room, where he sometimes takes my place during the session, projecting his ill part into me in a kind of *quid pro quo*. Charles would love to be a psychoanalyst; when he was about 15 years old, he had written a school essay on Freud.

Charles's relationship with his father was fraught with difficulty, and that was how I interpreted the sketch in which the car crashes into the father–tree. His rivalry was often expressed as aggressiveness towards a father who,

in reality, was quite flexible. Just as he liked taking the
place of the psychoanalyst, Charles would also take his
father's place—that of the ideal ego, to use Freud's term;
he disliked being the son or the patient. Sometimes he
did understand that as far as the analysis was concerned
he would have to learn the difficult job of "being a
patient". If he could succeed in this, he would be able to
share the same quest with me and my ego—patient and
analyst working as partners in the same adventure.

Charles became interested in archaeology. Freud, we
recall, felt that the metaphors of archaeology were ideally
suited to psychoanalytic work in its search for the ἀρκή.
Charles told me about restoring old houses and man-
sions, and he appeared to understand that we needed to
harmonize our research into the archaeology of the
present—i.e. the transference. The transference object is
not immutable, it changes with space and time and
according to the observing ego's perspective or vantage
point. The search for a space that we could share between
us—the transference space—is not a matter of simple
therapeutic curiosity concerning the inner world; it is a
prerequisite for the construction of the triad that struc-
tures the analyst–space–patient relationship. It is upon
this structure that the mental space of each partner will
be able to build. Charles would wonder about the meaning of clouds, shadows, form and shape, substance and
colour as they swam into his internal field of vision. He
was trying to understand what was going on inside his
head, and this could indicate that at such times he really
did feel that there was a space inside himself. He could
see, emerging into life, phenomena as yet without shape—
"shapeless" was Frances Tustin's (1986) term to describe
objects that do not yet have their own identity—things we
could try to understand together. What, in fact, he was
trying to do was to look at himself, to develop his observ-

ing ego in order to see himself through the eyes of his *alter ego*.

When he described what was happening inside his mental space, he talked of sensations, waves, vibrations of colour. In one of his drawings there is a "cosmic object" (see illustration on cover): Charles imagined rays of light coming out of a cave and rising into space. He added: "I'm thinking of black, red, and yellow: blots or rays." I commented: "With colours you're trying to describe, to transcribe your feelings. And you're trying to read what is written. Maybe you could go on a bit." Without hesitation, he continued: "Yes, black is despair, red is provocation, and yellow is hope." Then he added: "And blue is tranquillity. I'm trying to put all those colours together." I remarked: "Blue is the tranquillity you're looking for when you're in despair. Perhaps it is the provocative aspect in you or in others that keeps hope alive."

After a short pause, Charles mentioned another colour, which in Spanish is *morado*, corresponding to purple, which he confused with violet. He associated *morado* to *morada*, a house or dwelling-place. Psychotic patients use projective identification out of despair; it is equivalent to moving house, in that they try to get inside the other person and settle down there. As Bion said, the more their situation is persecutory and distressing, the further away their projections have to be. Charles's projections were sidereal; schizophrenics are particularly attracted to the cosmos—far from the difficulties of horizontality and the social interplay of everyday life in the present.

I reminded Charles that he had moved house when the family left Madrid for Paris. This change of domicile was an upsetting experience for all of them; for someone fragile, someone who had tremendous difficulty in inhabiting space and uniting his own fragments and shattered

bits and pieces, the experience could be traumatic.
Charles replied: "It's difficult. . . ." He hesitated, then went
on: "I'm thinking of the Arabs who invaded Spain." He
glanced at a painting representing a child holding the
reins of a wooden horse on wheels. This reminded him of
the Trojan horse, which he then drew (Figure 20). Since
the painting depicted a toy horse, there was some element
of playfulness in this sequence, a movement towards the
infantile ego. A delusional transference can make head-
way when the inhibited frozen child part begins to wake
up and warm up. Charles had certainly not forgotten how
to play. The purpose of the Trojan horse was to trick the
Trojans and thereby invade the city. Charles said: "In
Troy, nine cities are buried, it's private." I wondered what
"private" meant in this context; my view was that the
archaeological research he was doing with me was something very private. Charles comes from a family of nine;
perhaps they were interlocked inside one another, like
those Russian dolls. Either he was warning me, or saying
that the search for his origins, his primaeval language,
was something private.

We are here in the realm of the sacred and the secular;
we are all a *morada*, a temple. Charles associated *morada*
to moral, posing the ethical question of how to respect his
privacy. We know that in our work we have some power,
and the patient bestows even more power on us. This can
be a good thing, but it may also be a danger; it depends
on how the analysis develops. In accordance with the
primary process, Charles had condensed several ideas
and images into a single item or event.

There followed another short pause for reflection, then
Charles said: "Did you know there are affinities between
certain colours, and that colours can take the shape of
sounds or of voices?" This was his discreet way of re-

minding me that he still had hallucinations. How many colours, how many voices were speaking simultaneously inside Charles? "I'm thinking of geometrical figures, a dodecahedron." His attempt to find a language for himself had taken the form of not very well articulated geometrical figures; his thinking was trying to hack a passage through a mental space that was still unyielding and angular.

In one of his subsequent sessions, Charles gave me the impression of being cold and as hard as stone, as petrified and devitalized as I had felt him to be the first time we met. After our lively, colourful exchange, he had felt the need to draw back, to fortify himself again and put his armour back on. After a few moments, he said: "I'm thinking of white, it's a neutral colour", then added: "My mind's a blank" [*blanc*: white, in French], "I'm thinking of spies", he said, then, "I'm thinking of the Odyssey." I commented, "Last time, you spoke about your private language, and the session was intensely emotional. Maybe you feel you showed me too much of your private self. We spoke of ethics, too, so maybe you're suspicious of me, wondering whether I'm observing you with the aim of helping you or of spying on you. You're wondering who I am." "I'm thinking of yellow", said Charles—in his language, yellow means hope, so I added: "If we respect each other, there's hope. If we can wait a bit until the atmosphere between us becomes less of a threat, then we can go on hoping."

In another session, Charles drew a stony landscape scene. One of the rocks resembles a terrifying petrified bird (FIGURE 21). This is Nature's catatonia, the petrification of time, a lonely and desolate landscape. I can imagine Charles in such a universe, merging into hard and threatening Nature. When the ego is so fragile, the substance of which objects are made becomes vitally important: we may be made of stone, of wood like Pinocchio, of steel. These metaphors are the semantics of the materiality of human beings, and this is particularly important for psychotics. Looking at his sketch, I had the feeling that Charles would like to free himself from his condition as a lifeless bird and soar upwards into the blue.

In the following session, after a long, heavy silence, something strange occurred in me: I began to feel sluggish, as though in a state of lethargy, while Charles was far away, cut off, shut up in his own world. There was no life between us, no vibrations, no air, no wind—just as in the de Chirico townscapes I mentioned earlier. Suddenly, I imagined I could hear a bird sing. I wondered what was going on: was I having an hallucination? "Where is the bird?" I asked, and Charles, extricating himself from his stony mutism, replied, "In my stomach." I was still astonished and went on: "What does the bird want? Is it hungry? Cold?" A playful kind of transference stirred and woke me up. The atmosphere of the transference space had changed, becoming less catatonic and less threatening; there was space for the little bird, for that part of Charles's infantile ego outside narcissism, the part that was not stony, the part that needed help and warmth and food. The presence of an infantile ego, in Charles and in me, created a play-ground (Winnicott) and breathed life back into the archaeological research. When experience is petrified, the fragments produced when the psychic apparatus breaks down freeze and become confused; but when hardness melts, everything breathes—Nature and Charles's infantile ego give birth to a bird. This is not in itself sufficient: all is not yet in harmony, for the threatening voices re-appear and the noises of the city are again persecutory. The transference, in fact, is an alternating current—positive following negative, and vice-versa. Charles said, "Today my thoughts are shaped like thoughts." "What about sounds and noises?" I asked. "Just sounds and noises", was his reply.

I do think that Charles has improved, but at that point in the analysis a fundamental question came to the fore: the narcissistic wound. The pathological narcissism of his ego ideal—being the King of Spain, the delusion nourishing the idealized image and making it patholog-ical—was beginning to deflate. This is the phenomenon I call "narcissistic depression"—linked to the loss not of the object, but of a highly cathected part of the ego (cathected, that is, by the delusion). The delusional state of mind often feels crushed by the reality principle. In the narcissistic transference as described by Rosenfeld, the Other is the patient's opposite number, his mirror image, his shadow, his manufactured object. This prevents the narcissistic mind set from being imperilled. On the other hand, when a patient begins to be able to tolerate differ-ence and to think of the other person as distinct from himself, interplay and dialogue become possible; without difference, there is only echo. If the ego loses prestige, it may react negatively and attack linking. Two states of mind are then locked in combat: the desire to be helped, versus the desire to impose one's own pathological outlook/inlook. The ego becomes the battleground for political supremacy between the delusional part and the infantile ego seeking the help of an adult ego. The child and adult parts within the same person may try to nego-tiate through play, each allowing the other to challenge its basic tenets—a risky business, but if successful, dia-logue becomes possible. Space for *logos* can then expand, the possibility of enlightenment develops—a resplendent light, not a broken lamp like the one Charles had drawn at the start of his analysis. The remains of the cata-strophic experience that is a schizophrenic crisis contain some potential for warmth and light.

In his paper on narcissism, Freud (1914c) emphasized that the disposition to pathological narcissism is often accompanied by a tendency to exaggeration. The psychotic patient's ego becomes the centre of a solar system. Sometimes in the schizophrenic's mental space there are several galaxies, each with its own sun. When I look at Van Gogh's painting *Starry night* (FIGURE 22), I can see something that is both full of creative talent and impossibly insane. There are several planetary systems, and the moon is striving to eclipse the sun—this would make me think of the combined parents in cosmic conflict. Therein lies the "brave new world" of the psychotic crisis, a moment of intensely painful lucidity from which we may— or may not—be able to extricate ourselves. At the same time, it is a moment of light and warmth, which could bring immense benefit as long as circumstances are right and helping hands nearby. My impression is that Van Gogh's mental stability was quite satisfactory during the period he was living in Arles; when he left for Normandy, on the other hand, his condition worsened; it was as though his destructive part had begun attacking his linking capacity, and only the originality of his artistic ability remained.

In Charles's world, too, there were many sun-kings, many dissociated split-off kings, each locked up in autistic space, then suddenly exploding and making war on each other. This is the crisis situation, the watershed between the compartmentalized universe typical of more-or-less chronic schizophrenics and the potentialities of awakening. As the barriers of enclosure fall down, coming together is felt to be catastrophic; Heraclitus's war metaphor is an appropriate description. In the transference, as Bion (1966) remarked, such an experience may produce a spark of life that will prove vital for the therapeutic process. The sensation, blunted for so many years, that time

is once more in motion turns into a conflagration; coldness abruptly becomes heat. Charles had split his mighty
feudal ego into four parts, each of which claimed to be
king of the castle (the famous "multiple personality" of the
schizophrenic), and the battle was projected into the cosmos. In Van Gogh's painting, too, the battle is sidereal,
the atmosphere apocalyptic. The hope of the psychotic
ego is to invent a Messiah, a charismatic ego-guide, or
to put on the mantle of a Messiah and project outwards
the fragments of a mutilated disoriented universe, a
world desperately seeking direction. In Charles's case, the
struggle is between this psychotic project and the yellow
of another hope, the hope of help and understanding,
the hope of sharing with his psychoanalyst *inter alios* the
experience not only of death but also of life.

CHAPTER EIGHT

A space for concluding

N
ow that I am coming to the end of this volume, I would like to discuss in a little more detail the question of emptiness and absence. I wrote an article (Resnik, 1985a) with this very title in memory of David Liberman, a famous Argentinian psychoanalyst. He was a childhood friend of mine; his loss set in motion inside me all kinds of painful and nostalgic memories.

Remembering [*recordari*] is a way of evoking feelings. In Latin, *recordari* means to bring back to mind [*re*: back; *corda*: heart, mind]. This is quite different from Aristotle's reminiscence, which is sporadic, colder, and has more to do with reason and logic. In Aristotle's *Poetica*, memory is a recreative, lively mimesis. The Greek catharsis is at the root of many fundamental concepts of psychoanalysis— not only a liberation, but also re-creation, bringing back to mind.

Memory, evocation, and ritualization all have a part to play in the idea of tragedy, from the Greek τράγος [*tragos*: he-goat] and ῳδή [*aoide*: song]; hence the cult of Dionysus, in which catharsis is represented by sacrifice, the violent presence of a primal absence. Nietzsche would say that tragedy is born of the spirit of music, which, with its rhythm and harmony, encourages ritualization, sublimation, and re-creation of an absence in all of its aesthetic fullness.

Music, the art of Dionysus, generates energy, vigour, and liberty in life—in other words, internal movement and emotionality. To re-create is to play with a memory that has feeling; we play with memories to express what we are feeling and to reveal nostalgia.

Nostalgia is a turning homeward, νόστος [*nostos*] (in Homer, Odysseus thinking of Ithaca) with pain, ἄλγος [*algia*]. In suffering, the *algia* makes contact with the distant object of desire. By playing painfully with memories, we re-create life and rediscover the pleasure of being alive.

Let me transport you to Paris with me—to 20 rue Bonaparte, in the heart of the Latin Quarter, where I am waiting for a patient. I am waiting for Mr Duval, an old, melancholic child 50 years of age; I wrote about him in my book on the psychotic experience. He lives in a provincial town outside Paris and he travels into town every week and stays a few days in Paris for his four sessions. He lives with his mother—or, more accurately, "inside" his mother, consubstantially with her. She is his matter, his substance, as well as his *mater*.

One of his relatives accompanies him from his mother's house to the railway station, where an enormous "orange-coloured bottle" awaits him; this is the name he gives the train, devouring distances with its huge mouth—a carboy, as he puts it, impatient to unite the maternal home with Paris.

In his carboy on wheels, he is "bottled" from one body to another: from mother to train, from train to the Paris station. When he reaches Paris, he takes his "green bus"—again his term—to his hotel in Observatory Street, where he sometimes feels observed, watched, interpreted in an accusatory way by the "man with the stare", condemning his parasitic attachment, his adherence, to his mother. And so, one into the other, as in André Breton's game, he goes from his mother's body to the body of the train, the carboy, the green bus, his hotel, and, finally, to his session: moving continuously from one inside to another.

Mr Duval reaches 20 rue Bonaparte. I leave the door open and call out, "Come on in." "Yes, sir", he answers in a voice full of suffering, dragging along his forlorn body, an old–newborn baby attached to its feeding bottle. Even his age is a series of interlocking time sequences placed in layers one on top of the other; his personal chronology varies from 6 months to 72 years, his mother's age. His mother–body is an old cradle trailing sluggishly through space, from the streets of his home-town to Paris, from one extremity to the other, from his original *mater*–matter to the *mater analytica*, his psychoanalytic session. In the session, Mr Duval drops heavily down into rather than onto the couch; his desire is to live inside the object, rather than with it, typifying his maternal transference. After a gloomy, whimpering silence, he says in his usual slow and monotonous way, "It's difficult to leave my home-town. I'm thinking of my mother, the orange-coloured train. Now I'm thirsty, I'd like a glass of orangeade. . . . I'm thinking of a baby holding an orange in its hand, I'm thinking of a feeding-bottle. . . ."

He is, indeed, bottled, dressed in glass, like Cervantes' *Licenciado Vidriera*. "Do not touch, he might break. . . ." "I'm thinking of the orange-coloured sun", says Mr Duval after a long silence. "Of the reddish evening sun as it sinks to the horizon, dying, then coming to life again, day after day. . . ." As Phaethon, son of Helios the sun–father, drove the chariot of the orange-coloured sun in all its resplendent glory through the heavens and in his desire too close to the earth–mother.

"I'm thinking of the devil." The devil διάβολος [*Diabolos*: Satan] is the antagonist, the adversary who opposes father and mother. That little old devil–Duval opposes the pontifex–father [*pons*: a bridge, which both connects and separates], who says, "Enough is enough" to child and to mother; only then can they wean from each other and accept the bridge that straddles the abyss.

The antagonist–devil is his body refusing to go forward in case it falls down. In order to learn to walk, we must learn how to fall; one leg cushions the fall as the other loses balance. The flesh is antagonistic and refuses separation, while the spirit is willing and desires to come. The tension between refusal and willingness produces a struggle; the solution lies in the quest for equilibrium. His tired old body does not want to move, but his monotonous achromatic voice sometimes becomes alive and colourful, and he begins to think in colour: images and colours appear, the orange of the train, the green of the bus, yellow when he says, "I'm thinking of a lemon. . . . I can see the yellow leaves of the lemon-tree."

One day in school—a place I travel to with him in the metaphorical mobility of the transference—the schoolmistress makes her entry onto the stage. She is "leafing" through sheets of paper for a written examination. Mr Duval "leaves" his paper blank, then abruptly tears it into pieces and throws the fragments away. When the teacher asks him for his answer paper, he replies, "I don't have it." The teacher finds it, torn to shreds, and demands, "Who tore this paper?" Mr Duval accuses a classmate, who, of course, had nothing at all to do with the incident; it is only after a considerable lapse of time that Mr Duval admits his responsibility—his crime, as it were—and the iniquity of betraying his friend. Yet, by his devilish antagonistic act in intuitive opposition to his empathy, he finds an apparent solution to his problem, that of being away from home and separated from his mother: tearing up the sheet of paper and refusing to learn anything brings him back home, like a baby, to his *mater*–matter. It is as though the schoolteacher had said, "Very, well, if you don't want to learn, go back to your mummy", just as when a father tires of his child and tells him to go and talk to mummy (or vice-versa).

In Mr Duval's personal mythology, the tearing of the paper conceals a secondary gain: the return to maternal space, to endogamy as opposed to the paternal metaphor encouraging him to go forward into weaning, separation, and exogamy.

Fragmenting time, destroying space for absence, empty and lymphatic, devitalized, devoid of all experience of time, Mr Duval is drying up, becoming non-human, and losing all notion of what it might mean to feel alive inside. Feeling alive is quite different from mechanical incorporation, where experiences merely accumulate and occupy the totality of space, leaving no room for thinking.

The idea that one has an "inside", an inner world, is concomitant with the experience of time as a structured continuity; being alive includes being alive to suffering, and every separation is a little death. Mr Duval avoids grief in one of two ways: either he destroys and fragments time (hence emptying himself of all experience of time as a living structure), or else he evacuates loss into the external environment, which henceforth feels devoid of meaning and deprived of all vitality.

The result is that Mr Duval experiences reality as bleak and desolate, with no presence and no true absence, empty both inside and outside—a world in which it is impossible to be alive, in which authentic existence is inconceivable. Emptiness does not mean absence of feeling. When Melanie Klein was asked to describe emptiness, she told the story of how a little boy, coming into the therapy room for his session, declared: "It's empty here." He said it with fear in his voice, and this inspired Mrs Klein to ask him what "empty" meant for him; for this little boy, empty meant that the room was filled with demons, phantoms, hostile forces . . . empty, that is, of all possibility of empathy, reassurance, re-creation. In Kleinian terms, we would say empty of good objects.

In psychotics, and sometimes in non-psychotics, emptiness supplants absence as amnesia supplants memories. The same occurs when re-creating is too painful and persecutory. The child in us hates the absent parents, be they temporarily missing or gone for all time, i.e. dead. Every child is to some degree narcissistic and egocentric; he feels that his parents have no right to disappear, and his hatred is such that he cannot work though the process of mourning. Ancient Greek tragedy ritualized this aspect of mourning in the infantile ego of the spectators. The goat sacrifice enabled hatred and violence to be displaced so as to preserve the consecrated object. René Girard (1972), following Marcel Mauss, argues that the group ritualizes its hatred of the absent object loved ambivalently by displacing its aggressive feelings and sacrificing a scapegoat.

In chapter four, I spoke of one of my patients—Mr Tavel, who had lost his mother many years before but had been unable to carry through the work of mourning; he was very inhibited and emotionally handicapped. He had reminiscences, not memories, of his mother, and he was unable to re-create her with feeling and emotion. I argued that his dream of the "burial in reverse" of his mother had been a turning-point for the therapy. What had come back to him in a vivid, "living" memory of his dead mother was an object relationship with her, together with the part of himself that had suffered and had been buried with her to keep pain away, to avoid grief, and to bury his capacity to mourn. As he returned to his body with the funeral procession, Mr Tavel began to feel real emotions (inner movement) and anxiety—and these were no longer mere words to him. Frozen in time, he began to melt and dissolved in tears; time, once paralysed in space, began to flow again and to become emotionally meaningful.

Mr Tavel could henceforth recover some potential for experiencing absence, nostalgia, pain: he could take back into himself his feeling-ego. Accepting the pain of mourning enabled him to breathe life into devitalized aspects of his body and of his mental space, aspects he had hitherto not felt involved in.

He said one day: "Now I remember—*four Jews were leading the funeral procession.*" (Mr Tavel had four sessions per week.) The Jews were carrying the corpse of his dead mother, like the Jewish psychoanalyst who helped him to dis-cover, dis-inter, the feeling of absence, to open up to emptiness; now he could begin to work through the loss of the maternal object and the primary relationship with her. Mr Tavel was beginning to remember, to open doors . . . One memory led to another: "I remember when I was a boy", he said with emotion, "my childhood in the country. My mother's parents were farmers, she was a daughter of the soil. At that time, the soil was everything, it determined our very existence, mother nature. . . . Farming meant respecting the rhythm of the seasons."

The rhythm of the seasons is itself a procession, a ritual movement of nature. There was no option but to accept whatever became of the seeds that were sown; the soil was made ready for fertilization in the hope that it would bear fruit. Then man would continue his dialogue with nature, *homo naturalis* once more in partnership with Gaia.

"I remember", continued Mr Tavel, "that in the burial dream, *during the ceremonial procession back to the house, the priest threw a handful of earth on the coffin, as though he was throwing seed on the soil in order to re-create and give birth once more . . .*"—to re-create symbolically the absent object.

In my psychoanalytic practice, I try to respect each patient's personal rhythm; psychoanalysis means being able, in the transference relationship, to evoke past experience, re-live it, communicate it, and try to understand it. The Greek word εμπειρια is experience rather than experiment: it has to do with a living relationship, with all its sufferings and joys. There is no pleasure without pain, no pain without suffering. The analytic space, the *matrix*, is the *mater*–matter of the relationship, and the image of the father has an impact on what the analytic space in the maternal transference can contain; to contain is not in itself sufficient. To put the maternal space in order— every *corpus*, male or female, is maternal, said Meister Eckhart—a structuring axis is required, a paternal phallus, a spine, a father who can "vertebrate" disorder and "straighten things out": an internalized father in the physical and mental backbone of every human being.

I suggest a prelude to the idea of Oedipal and pre-Oedipal triangles: the linear triangle. The child goes from a primary symmetrical environment to partition and separation, and this first scission produces a triad: between the two poles lies the danger of falling into the abyss. The *pontifex*–father, owner and builder of bridges [*pons*], transforms the gaping mouth of the abyss—there is henceforth a place for linking and for crossing from one side to the other.

This would be my way of illustrating Melanie Klein's concept of the combined parents—not simply as an unconscious persecutory phantasy, but also as a fundamental metaphor for reconstruction. Once we are able to work through the mourning that individuation entails, we can learn to walk (to fall without hurting ourselves too much), to separate from the maternal body, to move about in the world.

Communication with the Other requires incorporation of experiences, patterns of object relations, figures, functions, value systems—all the building-blocks of our inner world and our external *persona*, the mask we wear. But accumulating and agglomerating experiences, paralysing them, deep-freezing them, evacuating them—this is no way to create the foundations for authentic intimacy. The inner world is a structural and dynamic concept, where the experience of time gives meaning and veracity to feelings: how we inhabit our body, how we can preserve the physical and mental verticality of *homo erectus*. The erect posture is a product of a harmonious interpretation of the world and of commerce with our environment [Heidegger's *Umgang*]; this, in turn, enables us to construct our own world, our own way of being, to acquire personal identity and uniqueness. To do this, we must set forth; to live is to learn while moving forward on our journey through life, accepting the passage of time and vertebrating the adventure, linking absence with presence, pause with *logos*.

I would like now to conclude this book with some thoughts on the concept of emptiness in Oriental philosophy. A book by François Cheng, *Vide et plein* (1979), had a major influence on my thinking; in it, the author points out that in Taoism the idea of "emptying one's self" is a way of creating a space for thinking with emotion. We could put this another way and say that creating inner space for oneself, or re-discovering it inside oneself, gives meaning, shape, and luminosity to life.

The second source of my reflection on this question is more personal. Near my home in Venice there is a glass-blower, a craftsman-cum-actor, constantly surrounded by spectators—spontaneously formed groups of admiring children and tourists—whom I often join. And the miracle occurs: from the creation of emptiness (air) within matter emerges the form and radiant luminosity of a precious object.

To develop insight, to look into our inner abyss, is a way of creating space for oneself, of making one's way (opening up) through the unknown labyrinth of unconscious corporeality. As we gradually overcome the vertigo that inevitably accompanies all inner discovery, looking inside manifests our willingness to learn, to discover, and to repair.

The issue in archaeology is how to reclaim and reconstruct a buried world in a space that must first be recaptured. This may be what inspired Heinrich Schliemann, the adventurous archaeologist who had the thrill of discovering the legendary site of the siege of Troy. The psychoanalytic adventure is an expedition in which the aim is to discover mental space, to imagine a *locus* that will give substance to long-lost thoughts and enable them to reassemble—to acquire a thinker, in Bion's words; the thinker is the psychic ego that has once more found place in the body ego. Neurotic patients, and above all borderline and psychotic patients who give greater importance in life to concrete events because they have so much difficulty with feeling and thinking, can through psychoanalysis try to discover the key to their internal world—internal, in contrast to the observing ego projected onto the external world. Everything depends on one's point of view, one's perspective. With good analysis, the observing ego, self-observation, the eye of the patient can improve its capacity to reflect; the analyst's eye becomes a place for thinking, for reflection–refraction, a window for looking into the internal cosmos. Reflection and thinking are like the interconnected mirrors in the Magritte painting; psychoanalysis is a quest for the internal world that is in inevitable conflict with the external world while at the same time striving to interact with it. The psychoanalyst can be the mediator, the metaphorical bridge between different aspects of reality. The quest for (self-)knowledge is often painful but vitally important and fascinating.

REFERENCES

Abbott, E. A. (1952). *Flatland.* Harmondsworth: Penguin Books.

Badaracco, J. G. (1986). Identification and Its Vicissitudes in the Psychoses: The Importance of the Concept of the "Maddening Object". *International Journal of Psycho-Analysis, 67* (2): 133 ff.

Bion, W. R. (1957). Differentiation of the Psychotic from the Non-Psychotic Personalities. *International Journal of Psycho-Analysis, 38.* [Reprinted in *Second Thoughts.* London: Karnac Books, 1984.]

Bion, W. R. (1966). Catastrophic Change. *Scientific Bulletin of the British Psycho-Analytical Society, 5.* [Reprinted in *Attention and Interpretation.* London: Karnac Books, 1984.]

Bonaparte, M. (1952). La légende des eaux sans fond. In: *Psychanalyse et biologie.* Paris: Presses Universitaires de France.

Charcot, J. M. (1893). *Clinique des maladies du système nerveux.* Paris: Progrès Médical.

Chaslin, Ph. (1920). *Psychiatrie: traité de pathologie médicale* (edited by E. Sergent). Paris: Maloine.

Cheng, F. (1979). *Vide et plein.* Paris: Seuil.

Ferenczi, S. (1909). Introjection and transference. In: *Jahrbuch der Psychoanalyse.* [Reprinted in *First Contributions to Psycho-Analysis.* London: Karnac Books, 1980.]

Festugière, A. J. (1936). *Contemplation et vie contemplative selon Platon.* Paris: Vrin.

Freud, S. (1912–13). *Totem and Taboo. S.E.,* 13, pp. xv, 1–161.

Freud, S. (1914c). On Narcissism: An Introduction. *S.E.,* 14, pp. 67–102.

Freud, S. (1915c). Instincts and their Vicissitudes. *S.E.,* 14, pp. 109–140.

Freud, S. (1917e [1915]). *Mourning and Melancholia, S.E.,* 14, pp. 237–258.

Freud, S. (1936a). Letter to Romain Rolland: "A Disturbance of Memory on the Acropolis". *S.E.,* 22, pp. 237–248.

Freud, S. (1940a [1938]). *An Outline of Psycho-Analysis. S.E.,* 23, pp. 139–207.

Friday, N. (1977). *My Mother, My Self.* New York: Dell Books.

Girard, R. (1972). *La violence et le sacré.* Paris: Grasset.

Heimann, P. (1952). Certain Functions of Introjection and Projection in Early Infancy. In: M. Klein, P. Heimann, S. Isaacs, & J. Riviere (Eds.), *Developments in Psychoanalysis.* London: Hogarth Press [reprinted London: Karnac Books & The Institute of Psycho-Analysis, 1989].

Isaacs, S. (1952). The Nature and Function of Phantasy. In: M. Klein, P. Heimann, S. Isaacs, & J. Riviere (Eds.), *Developments in Psychoanalysis.* London: Hogarth Press [reprinted London: Karnac Books & The Institute of Psycho-Analysis, 1989].

Janet, P. (1909). *Les névroses.* Paris: Flammarion.

Jones, E. (1953–1957). *The Life and Work of Sigmund Freud* (3 vols.). London: Hogarth Press.

Kaberry, P. (1963). An Evaluation of the Work of Malinowski. In: R. Firth (Ed.), *Man and Culture.* London: Routledge & Kegan Paul.

Klein, M. (1931). A Contribution to the Theory of Intellectual Inhibition. In: *Love, Guilt and Reparation and Other Works.* London: Hogarth Press, 1975 [reprinted London: Karnac Books & The Institute of Psycho-Analysis, 1992].

Klein, M. (1952). The Origins of Transference. In: *Envy, Gratitude and Other Works.* London: Hogarth Press, 1975 [reprinted London: Karnac Books & The Institute of Psycho-Analysis, 1993].

Klein, M. (1975). *The Psycho-Analysis of Children.* London: Hogarth Press.

Klein, M. (1963). On the Sense of Loneliness. In: *Envy, Gratitude and Other Works.* London: Hogarth Press, 1975 [reprinted London: Karnac Books & The Institute of Psycho-Analysis, 1993].

Laplanche, J., & Pontalis, J.-B. (1967). *The Language of Psychoanalysis.* London: Hogarth Press, 1973. Reprinted London: Karnac Books & The Institute of Psycho-Analysis, 1988.

Leroy, E. B. (1933). *Les visions du demi-sommeil (hallucinations hypnagogiques).* Paris: Alcan.

Lewin, K. (1963). *Field Theory in Social Science.* London: Tavistock.

Malinowski, B. (1944). *A Scientific Theory of Culture.* London: Chapel Hill.

Malinowski, B. (1964). *The Argonauts of the Western Pacific.* London: Routledge & Kegan Paul.

Matte-Blanco, I. (1975). *The Unconscious as Infinite Sets.* London: Duckworth.

McDougall, J. (1978). *Plaidoyer pour une certaine anormalité.* Paris: Gallimard. [*Plea for a Measure of Abnormality.* New York: International Universities Press, 1980.]

Pichon-Rivière, E. (1952). Quelques observations sur le transfert chez les patients psychotiques. *Revue Française de Psychanalyse, 16:* 1–2.

Pichon-Rivière, E. (1975). *El proceso grupal del psicoanalisis a la psicologia social.* Buenos Aires: Nueva Vision.

Reich, W. (1933). *Charakter Analyse.* Copenhagen: Sexpol Verlag. [*Character Analysis.* New York: Oregone Institute Press, 1950.]

Resnik, S. (1985a). El vacio y la ausencia. *Psicoanálisis, A.P. de B.A., 7* (1–2): 69.

Resnik, S. (1985b). La visibilité de l'inconscient. *Revue de Psychothérapie Psychanalytique de Groupe, 1–2.* [Reprinted as *La Visibilità dell'Inconscio.* Rome: Teda Edizioni, 1994.]

Resnik, S. (1986). *L'Esperienza Psicotica.* Turin: Bollati Boringhieri.

Resnik, S. (1989). El padre en el psicoanálisis. *Revista de Psicoanálisis, 4:* 499.

Rolland, R. (1931). *Empédocle d'Agrigente.* Paris: Albin Michel.

Rosenfeld, H. A. (1950). Notes on the Psychopathology of Confusional States in Chronic Schizophrenias. *International Journal of Psycho-Analysis, 31:* 132. Also in: *Psychotic States.* Reprinted London: Karnac Books, 1982.

Rosenfeld, H. A. (1987). *Impasse and Interpretation.* London: Tavistock.

Schilder, P. (1935). Space, Time, and Pereception. *International Journal of Psycho-Analysis, 16* (3): 366.

Searles, H. F. (1979). The Patient as Therapist to His Analyst. In: *Countertransference and Related Subjects.* New York: International Universities Press.

Tustin, F. (1986). *Autistic Barriers in Neurotic Patients.* London: Karnac Books.

Winnicott, D. W. (1958a). The Capacity to Be Alone. *International Journal of Psycho-Analysis, 39:* 416. Also in: *The Maturational Process and the Facilitating Environment.* Reprinted London: Karnac Books & The Institute of Psycho-Analysis, 1990.

Winnicott, D. W. (1958b). Primitive Emotional Development. In: *Through Paediatrics to Psycho-Analysis.* London: Tavistock [reprinted London: Karnac Books, 1992].

INDEX

as mirror, 16
persecutory, 41
mourning, 11, 20, 56, 107
for mother, 58-61, 104-106
movement:
as basis of change, 3
emotion as, 33
existence as, 4
fundamental to life, 4
and internal objects, 55
internal, and music, 100, 105
mental space in, 10, 35, 38
of planets, as discursive
rhythm of universe, 3
and shape of time, 34
stereotypical, 57, 62, 70
myth:
of cave, 4
link in global space, 10

narcissism, 8, 18, 96
narcissistic depression, 95
narcissistic transference, 95
narcissistic wound, 95
neurosis vs. psychosis, 67
Nietzsche, F., 100
nostalgia, 100

Odysseus, 100
Oedipus, 43
oneiroid states, and mental
space, 51–63
ontology of existence, xiii
Ostroff, Professor, xviii

pain, vs. suffering, 33
painting, and psychoanalysis, xiii
Paracelsus, 16
paranoid–schizoid position, 61
parental couple, role of, xiii
parents, combined, 107
Parmenides, 3, 20
personality, multiple, 97
Phaethon, 102
phenomenology, xiv
Philo of Alexandria, 16
philosophy, definition, 15

Pichon-Rivière, E. J., xiii, xviii,
19, 46
Plato, 4, 15
pleasure–unpleasure principle,
33
Plotinus, 16
Pontalis, J.-B., 16
projective identification, 8, 47,
70, 71
Klein's concept of, 7
pathological, 85, 88, 91
sadistic, 47
psychoses, 5, 24, 38, 66, 70, 79
concrete reality in, 67
hallucinations of, xiii
vs. non-psychosis, 24
psychosis vs. neurosis, 67
psychotic experience, 5, 28, 52,
100

reality, 66, 67
dialogue with, psychoanalytic
experience as, 8
dream, 65–76
and fantasy, 4, 54
flight from, 67
internal, 42
and external, 4, 34, 37, 38,
49
oneiric, 49
principle, 66, 67, 95
vs unreality principle, 65,
66, 67
psychic, 17, 35
psychotic experience of, 66
spatial, of body, 9
spatial dimension of, 4
transforming, 70
unexpected, 20
reflection–refraction, 109
Reich, W., 53
reminiscence, 99
and mourning, 11
vs. memory, 105
Resnik, A. Taquini, 3
Resnik, S., 4, 7, 10, 15, 28, 99
reverie, 39, 49